TEACHING
HIGH SCHOOL
ECONOMICS
The Analytical Approach

Pitman Education Series

Rychard Fink, GENERAL EDITOR

TEACHING
HIGH SCHOOL
ECONOMICS
The Analytical Approach

EDWARD C. PREHN

Pitman Publishing Corporation

New York / Toronto / London

Copyright © 1968 by Pitman Publishing Corporation
All rights reserved.
Library of Congress Catalog Number 68–14954
Manufactured in the United States of America
DESIGNED BY VINCENT TORRE

1.987654321

Preface

Of all the social studies, economics during the past two decades has received by far the most attention from educators. Curiously enough, the curricular spotlight has not been reflected adequately in the treatment given to economics by general-methods texts in the social studies published during this period. Thanks to the efforts of the Joint Council on Economic Education and its affiliated local councils and collegiate centers, a respectable body of thinking and accomplishment has accumulated, yet up to now no adequate methods handbook has appeared. Indeed, one would have to go back two generations for the last book specifically devoted to the teaching of high school economics.

It is very appropriate that the important task of writing a modern authoritative handbook for teaching economics has been assumed by Edward C. Prehn. With a long background in the economic-education movement, an even longer one as a teacher and chairman of economics, and as an author of a high school textbook and many articles in the field, Mr. Prehn is uniquely fitted to write *Teaching High School Economics*.

The beginning teacher, as well as the experienced one, will find in Mr. Prehn's volume a practical and skillful guide. It is well equipped with details and generalizations that should not only help to lighten the teacher's load, but also should show him the road to the joys of teaching today's analytical economics.

ALBERT ALEXANDER
Executive Director,
New York City Council on
Economic Education

Contents

PART I
The Economic Education Movement: Historical Background and Philosophy

PART II
Methods of Teaching the "New" Analytical Economics

CONTENTS

PART III

Preparation for Teaching Analytical Economics

Introduction

Teaching High School Economics: The Analytical Approach is designed to be used either as a basic textbook on high school methods in economics or as a supplement to one of the standard methods books in the social studies field. As a basic textbook, it encompasses all aspects of methodology. As a supplement, it places additional stress on analytical approaches to the teaching of economics and furnishes supplementary materials often omitted for lack of space in the customary single-chapter treatments.

Teaching High School Economics serves three purposes:

1. It is a short handbook on economics teaching for social studies teachers who have been assigned to teach the twelfth grade one-semester course in economics.

2. It is a convenient guide for laboratory-workshops given in conjunction with college-level courses, and is tailored to the specific needs of high school teachers and prospective teachers of economics.

3. It is a convenient summary of readily available resources which teachers can use to improve their own competency in economics and to enrich the economics course for their students.

A curriculum revolution is taking place in economic education largely under the aegis of the Joint Council on Economic Education, its Regional Councils, and its Collegiate Centers for Economic Education. This revolution has been characterized by the development of new curricula, more accurate and appropriate materials, and new teaching techniques. In order to comprehend the reasons for this revolution it is necessary to understand the dynamic post-World War II economic-education movement that triggered it. The economic-education movement is discussed in three introductory chapters in Part I, The Economic Education Movement: Historical Background and Philosophy. Part II, Methods of Teaching the "New" Analytical Economics, quite logically constitutes the bulk of the book. Part III, Preparation for Teaching Analytical Economics, tries to stimulate the faltering heart of the economic-education movement with a shot of educational adrenalin by supplying information and suggesting teaching materials that are useful to the novice and the seasoned teacher alike. The beginning teacher will find Chapter 4, The High School Economics Class: The Students and the Teacher, and Chapter 6, Planning the Economics Lesson, helpful. Hints for getting through that harrowing first day, suggestions for class management and discipline, and advice on long- and short-range lesson preparation are provided here for the tyro.

The author first became interested in writing *Teaching High School Economics* while he was writing his doctoral dissertation, "The Influence of the Economic Education Movement on the Public Schools of New York City, 1946–1966." He is indebted to Professors Richard F. W. Whittemore, Mary Ellen Oliverio, and Alice W. Spieseke, Teachers College, Columbia University, for their keen insights regarding newer approaches to the teaching of economics. Some of the methods and devices discussed in *Teaching High School Economics* were first described in the Teacher's Manual for *The Modern Economy in Action: An Analytical Approach* of which the writer is co-author with Albert Alexander, Executive Director of the New York City Council on Economic Education, and Arnold W. Sametz, Professor of Economics, New York University. Finally, much of the content of *Teaching High School Economics* is based on materials developed over the years by the author as a teacher of economics at Port Richmond High School and as chairman of social studies at New Dorp High School, both located in Staten Island, New York.

The author is grateful to Professor George G. Dawson, Head of the Social Studies Division and Director, Center for Economic Education, School of Education, New York University, for his helpful suggestions for the improvement of the book. He is especially indebted to Dr. Albert Alexander, who read the entire manuscript in its various stages of development and made valuable suggestions for its improvement. Any shortcomings of *Teaching High School Economics: The Analytical Approach*, however, are the sole responsibility of the author.

EDWARD C. PREHN

PART
I

The Economic-Education Movement: Historical Background and Philosophy

A curriculum revolution is taking place in economic education.

William E. Gardner &
Roman F. Warmke;
Social Education,
April 1966.

I *Economics in the Social Studies Curriculum*

Political Economy in Nineteenth-Century Secondary Schools

Political economy has been taught in the United States since the early days of the republic. Until after the Civil War, political economy on the college and secondary school levels was identical. Both levels used the same college textbooks, the content of which was drawn almost exclusively from treatises written in Great Britain. The courses stressed principles of production and distribution, with some attention to ethical questions. Vital issues of a controversial nature were included, but they were often discussed in a partisan manner.

"Political philosophy" was taught in Massachusetts from the very beginning of the American public high school. In 1821, it was prescribed in the English High School of Boston, and it was required from 1857 to 1898 in all large high schools in the state. Political economy was first taught in the high schools of New York State in the 1830's. After the Panic of 1837, the Reports of the New York State Regents show a marked increase in attention paid to the subject. Francis Wayland's *Elements of Political Economy, Abridged,* was the dominant text.

Before the turn of the century, secondary school political economy had assumed the general pattern, although not the specific content, which has characterized it ever since. Exchange and consumption were added to the earlier topics production and distribution, and the four topics constituted the main divisions of economics which were found in high school textbooks in some form or other down to the 1960's.

In practice, the study of political economy was focused on the sphere of the state and the role of the individual in the state, while economics as a social science viewed man's activities in the ordinary business of life with broader perspective. In 1884, the political economists of the United States organized the American Economic Association; in 1890 Alfred Marshall published his monumental neoclassical textbook, which he called *The Principles of Economics*, rather than *The Principles of Political Economy*. Thus, in keeping with trends which had been apparent for many years, the name of the subject was changed from *political economy* to *economics*.

High School Economics and the Professional Economist

Until quite recently, professional economists and teachers of economics in colleges and universities had not been interested in the teaching of economics below the college level. The American Economic Association occasionally included in its annual meetings papers and discussions on the problems of teaching the high school economics course, but took no official action prior to 1961. Until then, unlike historians, geographers, and political scientists, professional economists as a group had never become sufficiently interested in the teaching of their subject to name a committee to study high school practices and to make recommendations. Some professors of economics contended that economics was too scientific, too analytical, too theoretical, and too remote for high school students to comprehend. In 1894, the Committee of Ten of the National Education Association recommended that economics be included with civics and history rather than offered as a separate subject, but this position was contested by such leading economists of the period as Professor John R. Commons and Frank Taussig. The NEA *Proceedings* of 1901 also contain articles in favor of teaching economics as a separate high school discipline.

Trends in Economic Education in the 1930's

Contemporary emphasis on economic education had its origin during the Great Depression of the 1930's. The controversial policies of the New Deal intensified interest in the study of economics on all educational levels. In 1938, the National Education Association set the objectives of "economic efficiency" and "economic literacy" as goals of the high school in *The Purposes of Education in American Democracy*. One of the outcomes of the depression was the virtual abolition of child labor in the United States, and as children of varying ability levels entered high school and remained to graduate the traditional liberal arts approach to economics was increasingly in question. The change in the size and the composition of the school population brought with it changes in curriculum, methodology, and materials.

Certain current trends in economic education on the high school level were apparent before World War II. Perhaps the most pervasive of these was the remarkable growth in consumer economics, which infused the high school economics course with a consumer-oriented, personal-problems approach that has remained down to the present.

A second trend was an attempt to place economics in its social setting. Over the years, the field of economics has steadily broadened to include sociology, economic history, and political science. In some instances, this process has accompanied a fusion of economics with other social studies. This trend has been perpetuated in our contemporary Problems of American Democracy course and is discernible in economics courses in the late 1960's.

A third trend has been the attempt to make economics more functional and more realistic by placing major emphasis upon problems which are within the everyday experiences of the students. Learning activities were broadened to include visual education, practical investigations, field trips, and the use of mass media, including radio; and textbooks provided challenging end-of-chapter materials (problems for further study, readings, "things to do") which attempt to involve the students.

The Status of Economic Education at Mid-Century

One reason that economics did not receive more attention as a distinct subject offering in the traditional high school curriculum until the 1960's was the weight of tradition itself. Someone once said, "It is easier to move a cemetery than to accomplish changes in curriculum." Economics has never enjoyed a position of status in high school. It was not generally a requirement for graduation; it was not a prerequisite for college entrance; and it did not lead to scholarships, advanced placement, or other awards and honors. In short it had little drawing power, especially for college preparatory students.

Early in the nineteenth century, after reading Thomas Malthus' *Essay on Population*, Thomas Carlyle dubbed economics "the dismal science." The nickname stuck, not because Malthus reached extremely dire conclusions regarding the economic future of mankind, but because successive generations of high school and college students have found the course in the "principles of economics," as it has been traditionally taught, a far from exciting subject. Prospective teachers skip economics during their pre-service training for many reasons—competing course requirements, more attractive electives, lack of awareness or interest, failure of schools to require or recommend it, and the image of economics as theoretical, dry as dust, and "the worst-taught course in American colleges and universities." In a classic report of the American Economic Association, the Committee on Undergraduate Teaching of Economics said, "A specter is haunting teachers of economics, the specter of bad teaching." [1]

Furthermore, economics was not required for a social studies major in most teacher-training institutions. Consequently, most social studies teachers were professionally trained in history, political science, geography, and even in anthropology and sociology, but there have been few teachers who were either interested in, or qualified to teach, economics. Furthermore, the growing holding power of our high schools increased the number of students not headed toward college and not interested in or seemingly able to profit from the traditional liberal arts economics course.

In the middle of the 1960's, there were in the United States over 12.1 million high school students, 60,000 social studies teachers and 45,000 teachers of business education. But only 20 percent of our high school students—some 400,000 young men and women—were receiving a separate course in economics. While more large school systems were offering an elective course in economics, only about 20 percent were requiring such a course. In general, electives tend to draw low registrations, particularly in economics. Perhaps equally important was the fact that most of our large school systems were teaching bits and pieces of economics at various points in grades 1 through 12. Qualitatively, however, how good was the economics which was being taught in the late 1960's? Only twenty-two states in the nation required a formal economics course or courses for the certification of social studies teachers. Further, the agitation about "economic illiteracy" brought home to an increasing number of teachers the disturbing fact that they are economically illiterate themselves. Scarcely any of them had majored in economics in college and only one half of the social studies staff had had as much as a single course in college economics.

[1] "The Teaching of Undergraduate Economics," Report of the Committee on Undergraduate Teaching of Economics and the Training of Economists, *American Economic Review*, Part 2, Supplement (December 1950), p. 1.

Obstacles to Effective Economic Education

There were several major obstacles to American economic education (or economic literacy) in the middle of the twentieth century. Some of these handicaps will doubtlessly remain with us for some time.

First, there was a shortage of qualified economics teachers. *Economic Literacy for Americans*, a report sponsored by the Committee for Economic Development in 1962, stated that only two out of nine social studies teachers were adequately prepared in economics—that is, could offer the six college credits in economics which have been recommended as minimal by the National Task Force.

Second, there was disagreement on aims and objectives. Until the National Task Force Report was issued in September 1961, there was no generally accepted standard for the kind of economics that could and should be taught in high school. This condition existed despite the efforts of the National Association of Secondary School Principals, the National Council for the Social Studies, and the Joint Council on Economic Education and its affiliates. Without widely accepted goals for economic education, the lack of standardized achievements tests for checking progress was not unnatural. Although many business, agricultural, labor, and educational groups had promoted economic education in the past, their efforts were usually uncoordinated and sometimes misdirected.

Third, textbooks in economics on the high school level were sometimes a generation behind economic scholarship. As a consequence, many economics teachers were teaching the economics of the 1930's in the 1960's, and, despite the Report of the National Task Force, some probably still are doing so. In the United States the textbook usually determines the course of study for subject areas in which teachers are inadequately trained or lack confidence. Good unbiased teaching materials were hard to come by. The booklets issued by the National Association of Manufacturers and the AFL-CIO reflected definite points of view. Even in the present decade, the Materials Evaluation Committee of the National Task Force could recommend less than two hundred items out of seven thousand it examined.

In essence, the economic-education movement in the United States since World War II has been engaged in a massive effort to remove these three major obstacles to nationwide economic literacy.

2 The Curriculum Revolution in Economics

The "New" High School Economics

Although the question of economics in the schools had been explored since the latter part of the nineteenth century, the need for new emphases in high school economics did not become apparent until after World War II. Advances in scholarship, new perspectives in the social sciences, and general acceptance of the "new" economics by the economics profession, leading businessmen, and responsible government officials made pre-war high school economics courses obsolete. The field of economics had changed so rapidly that even the best college courses of a few years before proved inadequate as preparation for teaching high school students in the late 1960's. Further, few social studies teachers had taken a quality course in economics at any time in their education.[1] Educators asked, How can teachers who are ill-at-ease, out-of-date, unaware of the implications of fiscal and monetary policy, or wrong in their understanding of basic economic principles be expected to make an effective response to the drive for economic literacy?

In part, the need for an analytical approach to teaching economics in high school, based on models and structure, was suggested by the wave of curricular reform that began in mathematics and the natural sciences in the middle of the 1950's. In part, the new approach also represented an attempt to apply to high school economics the learning theories of Jerome S. Bruner and others who had given teachers deeper insights into the learning process. And, in part, it was designed to pro-

[1] John R. Coleman, "When Secondary School Teacher and College Economist Meet," *The Bulletin of the National Association of Secondary School Principals* (November 1965), pp. 67–68.

vide the analytical tools needed today by the average American citizen for rational decision-making both in the marketplace and the polling place.

The Need for Better Economic Education

In a free, flexible, and dynamic society such as ours, the way in which the individual allocates his personal resources of time, talent, and money has a direct effect on the health of the economy and the status of the economy usually has an effect—often a profound effect—on the individual. Furthermore, the ordinary citizen must be able to distinguish inherited myths from contemporary realities. Much of our conventional economic wisdom has been distilled from experiences with life during an agrarian era. Too often we still subject economic facts to a prefabricated set of interpretations. For thus we can enjoy "the comfort of opinion without the discomfort of thought." [2]

These are some of the factors that have caused thinking citizens to ask, Are our teachers in elementary and secondary schools adequately trained in economic analysis to do their job? Can they communicate necessary basic understandings to future citizens? Is the case for economic education inseparable from the case for the survival of democratic capitalism?

The advocates of economic education have argued that economic literacy is vital to meet the challenges we are encountering in world markets of goods and ideas. As a consumer, worker, and voter, the average person today is called upon to make decisions which affect the welfare of all. In the final analysis, the effectiveness of democratic government depends on the capacity and the understanding of the people. For it is "the people who, through their votes and other influences, determine within broad limits the scope and nature of government policies." [3] *Economic literacy can be defined as the possession of basic understandings and skills needed by all individuals for intelligent management of their own business and financial affairs and for responsible participation as citizens in the determination of public policy and the maintenance of the general welfare.*

[2] President John F. Kennedy's Yale University Address.
[3] National Task Force on Economic Education, *Economic Education in the Schools.* New York, Committee for Economic Development, 1961, pp. 7–8.

The Economic-Education Movement

In the light of this definition, a good case can be made for the charge that many Americans were functional economic illiterates prior to the 1960's, and many still are such near the end of the decade. The post-World War II decades witnessed a growing interest in economic education by people in industry, education, government, and labor. This groundswell can be largely attributed to fresh assessment of the importance of an economically literate citizenry and to a widespread conviction that the study of economics was being neglected by the public schools and teacher-training institutions. The economic-education movement is uniquely American. While it is true that economics is a major subject behind the Iron Curtain, it serves only as a handmaiden to the political dogma of the monolithic state.[4]

Since 1949, the Joint Council on Economic Education, a nonprofit educational organization, has provided national leadership for the economic-education movement. Financed initially by the Committee for Economic Development, it has since the early 1950's been aimed primarily at the secondary schools of the nation. Within the Joint Council itself, leadership comes from educators, economists, businessmen, labor leaders, and farm groups. Financial support comes largely from national foundations and the business community. In 1967, the Joint Council's budget totaled $750,000, but this does not include DEEP funds originally estimated at $1.8 million for a five-year period. It is safe to say that over $5 million annually is going into economic-education efforts.[5] The Joint Council is the only organization in the economic-education movement that is formally affiliated with the American Economic Association and professional groups within the National Education Association, such as the National Association of Secondary School Principals and the National Council for the Social Studies, that are deeply concerned with economic education.

Forty-five affiliated State and Regional Councils on Economic Education, organized as a network and relying on independent fund-raising, carry on the Joint Council's mission on the local level. Thirty-three Centers for Economic Education on college and university campuses assist with research, publications, teacher-training, materials development, evaluation, and testing. In a sense, the Councils and the Centers reinforce and complement each other.

Slow to get off the ground during its first decade, the drive for more

[4] Editorial, "Economic Education," *Challenge: The Magazine of Economic Affairs,* 12:1 (March 1964).

[5] Haig Babian, "Economic Education: How It Began and Why," *Challenge: The Magazine of Economic Affairs,* 12:2–4 (March 1964).

and better economic education in the schools gained impetus with the publication of *Economic Education in the Schools,* the Report of the National Task Force on Economic Education (September 1961). The Task Force Report focused on those principles of economics which must be understood if citizens are to make wise decisions as voters. Other landmarks in Joint Council history include the 1962 television course, "The American Economy," sponsored by the American Economic Association, Learning Resources Institute, and the Joint Council. The economics lessons, taught by Professor John R. Coleman, were carried five times weekly for 32 weeks by the CBS Television Network and 59 ETV stations during 1962–1963 with a record daily audience officially estimated at over one million viewers. "The American Economy" series cost $1.3 million, plus an unknown additional amount donated by CBS. Kinescopes of "The American Economy" are still being viewed by more than five thousand teachers annually and screened in hundreds of secondary school classrooms. The Joint Council's Committee on Measurement of Economic Understanding completed the first *Test on Economic Understanding* based on national norms in 1963. It was published by Science Associates, Inc. in 1964.

Developmental Economic Education Program (DEEP)

The Joint Council's most ambitious project was a five-year Developmental Economic Education Program (DEEP) to develop prototype economic-education programs for kindergarten through twelfth grade. In 1967 one-third of the Joint Council's budget was earmarked for DEEP, then in its third year. DEEP is a cooperative endeavor of the Joint Council, the affiliated councils, consulting economists, colleges and universities, and the local school systems.

The Joint Council provided each DEEP school system with a financial grant, consultant time, a library of films of "The American Economy" television series, and an opportunity for an exchange of information at national meetings of DEEP coordinators and through *Deep Ideas,* the *J.C.E.E. Newsletter,* and other publications. For its part, each DEEP school system appointed a project coordinator, initiated a teacher-training program, appointed policy, curriculum, and community advisory committees, and shared experimental materials with other DEEP and cooperating school systems. The local affiliated Councils on Economic Education furnished consultant assistance and educational specialists.

During 1965–1966 over forty-five hundred teachers were provided with some formal training in economics. Teaching guides and learning materials for students are expected to be important by-products of the DEEP effort. At one time or another, twenty-nine school systems, including two Roman Catholic systems, were involved in the experiment, which has been called the largest of its kind in the behavioral-science field.

Community-oriented, community-managed, and community-supported, and directed by local educators, the economic-education movement has made significant progress during the 1960's. While economics has not achieved the status enjoyed by the sciences, mathematics, or American history in the high schools, there is ample evidence that the movement is achieving its basic goal—to increase economic understanding. More and better economics is being taught, methods and materials are improving, and through thousands of workshops and in-service courses teachers are being provided with greater knowledge and know-how in economics.

The Mid-Century Revolution in Economics

The economic-education movement was a product of the times. The lives of the people of our own country, and indeed of the whole world, changed with bewildering rapidity during the first six decades of the twentieth century. Increased productivity, a galloping technology, miraculous progress in the age-old war on grinding poverty, a world-wide ideological economic and political struggle between totalitarian communism and the free economies, and the transformation of the United States into the greatest political and economic power on earth stimulated further changes. Newspapers and periodicals reminded us of "the explosion of knowledge," "the population explosion," "the shrinking world," and the world-wide "revolution of rising expectations."

Partly because of dramatic twentieth-century developments such as these, a quiet, almost imperceptible, but nevertheless far-reaching revolution occurred in economics. A host of new developments in the field, such as the concept of the dual economy and the welfare state, stress on econometrics, linear programming, and above all the Keynesian Revolution, wrought changes in economic thought during the three decades which followed the Great Depression.

The Keynesian Revolution

The revolution in economic thought since the Great Depression of the 1930's was chiefly the result of the influence of a controversial British economist, John Maynard Keynes, whose *General Theory of Employment, Interest and Money* is one of the important books of the twentieth century. Before Keynes, classical economists assumed that the economy, if left to itself, would find equilibrium or stability through what Adam Smith called "the invisible hand." The invisible hand was self-interest, which brought all economic forces into balance and used them fully. For example, if wages rose too fast, Adam Smith argued, employers would lay off workers until wage stability returned. The same economic laws applied to capital and land, the other primary factors of production. Keynes pointed out that the automatic stabilizers in which classical economists placed their faith could actually aggravate rather than prevent a depression. Instead, he stressed the crucial role of the total purchasing power of the economy, exercised through aggregate demand. By aggregate demand he meant the total of all demand in the economy—demand for consumption and demand for investment, for both public and private purposes. Keynes believed that the prime goal of any economy is to achieve full employment. By full employment he meant the full use of resources and machines as well as men. He insisted that the only way to revive aggregate demand during a depression was for the government to cut taxes, reduce interest rates, and spend more heavily. Such policies involve ignoring government deficits. Keynesian theory implies that the government must fill the gap between savings and investment by means of public compensatory spending if it wishes to maintain a full-employment level of income. In short, compensatory spending requires the government to make up the difference between current spending by the private sector and spending which is needed to maintain full employment.

Keynes built his entire theoretical structure on an increasing tendency for people in an affluent society to save. While it is true that a wealthy person will erect an expensive country home, build a heated swimming pool, buy a luxurious yacht and, in general, consume more as his income increases, his consumption expenditures will be a smaller proportion of his income. In short, his tendency—Keynes calls it his "propensity"—to consume grows weaker while his propensity to save grows stronger. At high-income levels, opportunities for profitable investment may not suffice to absorb all savings.

The Employment Act of 1946

During World War II, the American economy demonstrated its astounding productive potential under the stimulation of government purchasing, financing, and selective controls. Despite this miracle of production, however, the old anxieties returned with the close of hostilities. The twenty-year interlude of boom and bust between the First and Second World Wars had shown the need for a new political apparatus for dealing with the economic problems of modern industrialism. The courageous ad hoc experimentation of the New Deal, supplemented by the scholarly probings of the Temporary National Economic Committee of 1938–1941, had pointed the way toward an expanded role for government in American economic life. With the hardships of the Great Depression of the 1930's still painfully in mind, many citizens now asked apprehensively, Can a post-war depression be avoided? Is it possible to maintain an expanding economy in a free society? What responsibility can and should the government assume for economic growth and stability?

Even before VJ Day, the research divisions of our major private and public agencies earnestly applied themselves to persistent and pressing economic problems. The National Bureau for Economic Research, the Committee for Economic Development, the National Planning Association, the Twentieth Century Fund, the Brookings Institution, the National Industrial Conference Board, the Congress of Industrial Organizations, the American Federation of Labor, the Federal Reserve Banks, and several governmental agencies were deeply involved. Committees in both houses of Congress attempted to draft legislation that would incorporate the wisdom acquired from the depression, the New Deal, and the war years. The Employment Act of 1946 formally declared that the major economic goals of our nation are full employment, maximum production, and high purchasing power, and that the federal government should see that all three are maintained for the economic well-being of the nation. This short and uncomplicated statute has been aptly referred to as "an economic constitution" for the United States.[6]

The Employment Act of 1946 established a Council of Economic Advisers to the President, its responsibility being to analyze economic trends in the United States and to recommend to the President policies designed both to foster full employment with price stability and to promote economic growth. The "Era of Economic Understanding" ushered in by the Employment Act of 1946 demanded of all an increasing matu-

[6] Edwin G. Nourse, "Current Aspects of Our Persistent Economic Problems," *Social Education*, 30:234–235 (April 1966).

rity of thinking in economics. By the Employment Act and the logic of circumstances "economic policy became everybody's business, and, by the same token, a significant sector of citizenship education." [7]

Since President Truman signed the Employment Act of 1946, the role of the federal government in economic life has expanded substantially. The social sciences have been used both in arriving at economic policies and in implementing economic programs. Political leaders have relied on the counsel of economists as never before and professional economists have become highly influential in the determination of public policy. Indeed, it is good politics for a politician to consult reputable economists who share his general political philosophy. In his annual report to the Congress and to the people, the President has been setting specific goals and proposing means of reaching them—means that are spelled out further in his budget and special messages. As a consequence, the need for economic literacy has become ever more urgent.

The Dual Economy of the 1960's

Because of World War II, a dual economy emerged in the United States as both government and private enterprise played a vital role in American economic life. What economists once expounded as a price-organized society became a price-and-tax-organized society. Fiscal policy and action assumed new importance, if not primacy. Some twenty years after his death, Keynes' theories were a major influence on the world's free economies and especially on our own, the richest and the most expansionist. In Washington the men who formulate America's economic policies used Keynesian principles not only to avoid the violent business cycles of pre-World War II days but to produce a phenomenal growth rate with relatively stable prices.

In *A Thousand Days*, Arthur Schlesinger Jr. stated that John F. Kennedy was "unquestionably the first Keynesian President." Not only did the Kennedy and the Johnson Administration accept Keynesian fiscal policy as an antidepression weapon, but both used it as a tool to support economic growth and to encourage the increasing welfare outlays of the Great Society programs. In fact, the income tax cut of 1964 was designed primarily to bolster and prolong recovery, not to combat incipient recession.

[7] G. Derwood Baker, "Educating Citizens for Economic Effectiveness, 1960–1980," *Citizenship and a Free Society: Education for the Future*, Franklin Patterson (ed.), Thirtieth Yearbook, National Council for the Social Studies, Washington, D.C., 1960, p. 126.

Structure

The "new" economics of the late 1960's is characterized by an analytical approach, the use of models, attention to the tools of the economist, and emphasis on the structure of the discipline. Indeed, the terms "structure" and "the 'new' economics" are often uttered in the same breath. "Structure" is a forbidding term to the uninitiated, since there is still no consensus about its meaning. Some social studies experts identify structure with generalizations drawn from the social sciences. Others equate structure with major concepts. In *Teaching the New Social Studies in Secondary Schools: An Inductive Approach,* Edwin Fenton defines it as "the analytical questions which historians and social scientists put to data in order to make it meaningful." To the layman, structure signifies the conceptual framework, the generalizations, the principles—in short, the abstractions of economics.

One important aspect of the structure of economics is the division of the discipline into two main parts: macroeconomics and microeconomics. Macroeconomics studies totals—total employment, total consumption, total investment, and national output. It is concerned with the problems of economic aggregates or the determination of the level of income and employment in the economy as a whole. Microeconomics, on the other hand, studies the small or the particular—the details of the economic process, that is, the fitting together of its various parts. The "parts" usually cluster about, or center in, the problems of pricing goods and of productive factors.

As a scientific discipline, economics is characterized by its social point of view, its objectivity, and its abstract nature. Abstraction is, of course, a common characteristic of all the sciences. As social scientists, economists continually search for system and order in the welter of facts and experiences that constitute the real world. By identifying underlying regularities, economists hope to simplify, systematize, and understand the essential nature of economic behavior and the factors that govern it.

In *The Process of Education,* Jerome S. Bruner, the Harvard psychologist and expert on learning theory, states that if the primary purpose of teaching is maximum usefulness of the subject to the student, the fundamental structure of the discipline must be taught. "To learn structure, in short, is to learn how things are related," he asserts. Unless a particular idea or topic can be meaningfully related to the fundamental structure of economics as a scholarly discipline, it does not belong in the course, according to Bruner. Specialists in economic education argue that a separate course, usually given in one of the semesters of the senior year in high school, is needed as a capstone to fix the structure in the minds of the students.

George Bernard Shaw was in error when he quipped that even if all the economists in the world were laid end to end they still would not reach a conclusion. Economists agree on what constitutes the conceptual framework or structure of their discipline, that is, the fundamental concepts and principles to which all economists, whether politically conservative or liberal, subscribe. Laurence Leamer has succinctly summarized the structure of economics under six main headings: the economic problem; production and its determinants; allocation of resources and economic choice; economic systems; microeconomic systems of flows, including exchanges, markets, and prices; and macroeconomic systems of flows.[8]

1. *The economic problem.* The economic problem (scarcity) considers the dilemma created by nature's limited resources vis-à-vis man's unlimited wants. It is the central core of economics. Ben W. Lewis says that the economic problem involves mankind in a never-ending task which reaches back to "the dim shadows of the past, and stretches endlessly into the future."[9] There is no solution to the economic problem and no relief from the everlasting task it imposes. The nature and extent of the task of coping with scarcity is touched on under the next three headings.

2. *Production and its determinants.* Production involves converting scarce resources into the goods and services mankind desires. Its determinants include the role of savings, investment, capital formation, and the organization of industry in the interests of efficiency.

3. *Allocation of resources and economic choice.* To "economize" means to allocate scarce resources to the best possible use through the opportunity-cost principle.[10] "The essence of economics," in the words of the Task Force, "is the necessity to choose among alternatives." There is never enough to satisfy all human wants.

4. *Economic systems.* To cope with the economic problem through increased productivity on the part of producers involves socioeconomic organization—that is, an economic system. The concept of an economic

[8] Laurence E. Leamer, *The Economist as Teacher: Informal Essays on the Collegiate Teaching of Economics*, Monograph C-12. Cincinnati, South-Western Publishing Co., 1965, pp. 9–11.

[9] Ben W. Lewis, "Economics," *The Social Studies and the Social Sciences.* New York, Harcourt, Brace & World, Inc., 1962, p. 110n.

[10] The opportunity-cost principle recognizes that, since all societies are faced with the problem of scarcity, decisions must be made concerning alternative uses to which scarce resources can be put. For example, if a piece of land is used for a skating rink, it cannot be used for a new school. The cost of a ski weekend is the cost of the tape recorder you could have bought. In the process of making choices between desirable alternatives, *opportunity costs* are incurred. In short, the cost of anything can be measured in terms of the most wanted alternative *foregone.*

system is one of the most important abstractions developed by the economist. Its purposes, rationale, and dynamic concerns, as well as the structure and operation of its major institutions, constitute the heart of economic understandings. Its oneness is illustrated by the interrelationships of economic forces and institutions.

5. *Microeconomic systems of flows, including exchanges, markets, and prices.* Although the classical economists tried to view economic forces with wide vision, they did not have the statistical data and the tools, including the computer, to do the job. Consequently, they tended to specialize: Adam Smith focused on the marketplace, Malthus on population, Ricardo on rent, Say on consumption, Marx on labor and wages, and Mill on distribution. Economists today call such specializations *microeconomics*. This portion of the fundamental structure of economics applies chiefly to private-enterprise economies. Microeconomics today is concerned with market quantities—for example, the output of the Tom Thumb Toy Company, the price of bagels in New York City, and the wages of bus drivers in Albany. Before World War I, the problems of microeconomics were the main concern of economists.

6. *Macroeconomic systems of flows.* John Maynard Keynes was the precursor of what economists today call macroeconomics (from the Greek *makros*, large or extended). Keynes thought that the way to understand the economy was to measure all "the myriad forces tugging and pulling at it"—national output, total employment, total investment, and total consumption. Macroeconomics is associated with national-income accounting (GNP and its numerous cousins, such as NI, PI, and NNI). Macroeconomics also brings to mind fiscal measures, international-trade policies, the general price level, interest rates, profits, and the determinants of income and its distribution. Since the 1920's, the main concern of economists has been the study of macroeconomics.

Some economists maintain that modern economics is not "either-or," but that it is a mixture of microeconomics and macroeconomics. It employs both the "micro" theories of Alfred Marshall and his neoclassical followers and the "macro" theories of John Maynard Keynes.[11] A course in economic theory concerns the study of both. The "new" economics, however, is the result of exciting developments in the macro field.

The six headings above outline the structure of economics—the hard core of the college principles course. This structure is the basic conceptual framework of the high school course in analytical economics

[11] The neoclassical school of economic thought, often associated with Alfred Marshall, was developed by leading British and American economists between 1870 and 1930. The neoclassical economists refined the economic concepts and analyses found in the works of the classical school of economists.

recommended by *Economic Education in the Schools,* the Report of the National Task Force on Economic Education. The emphasis placed by the National Task Force on analytical concepts, student analysis, and "the replacement of emotional, unreasoned judgments by objective rational analysis" is discussed in Chapter 7, "The Analytical Approach and the 'New' Economics." The Task Force suggests the following content for high school economics: an overview of the economic system; what the economy produces, and how; economic growth and stability; the distribution of income; and comparative economic systems. The Task Force Report merely furnishes guidelines, however; it is not a textbook nor a course of study for a one-semester high school economics course.

The Necessity for Economic Education

Edwin G. Nourse, the first chairman of the Council of Economic Advisers, cautioned Americans that our country more than ever needs thoughtful and enlightened citizens who have had economics courses in high school and college. Economic education, he argues, provides the tools of analysis and reasoning which our citizens "must have in order to be counted upon to help solve the problems that will persist in their adult lives." [12]

[12] Nourse, *op. cit.*, p. 235.

3 Approaches to Economic Education

The Social Studies and the Social Sciences

On the high school level economics is one of the social studies—the subjects which deal with the organization and development of human society and man as a member of that society. In *The Social Studies and the Social Sciences*, Lewis Paul Todd tells us that "the social studies are concerned with the whole life of man, with the past, the present, and the future that we 'now see through a glass darkly.'"[1] The term "social studies" is an umbrella for a group of high school subjects that deal with man in his social environment: history, government, sociology, economic and world geography, and, of course, economics. The term "social studies" dates from 1905, when Jesse O. Jones of Hampton Institute first applied the appellation to these subjects. In 1916, the National Education Association adopted the designation social studies because it met a definite semantic need. Although the social studies are taught, as formerly, as separate subjects, they also constitute a field, a loose federation, a distinct area of the high school curriculum.

On the college level, economics is one of the social sciences. The social sciences are devoted to the scholarly, detailed, logical study of human beings and their interrelations. A monograph titled "Theories of the Firm, Marginalist, Behavioral, Managerial" exemplifies the way in which the social sciences organize knowledge about human relationships in the economic sphere and use the methods of research for arriving at new knowledge. The social sciences concentrate on the basic concepts, assumptions, and interrelations that economists call *structure*. An

---

[1] The American Council of Learned Societies and the National Council for the Social Studies, *The Social Studies and the Social Sciences*. New York, Harcourt, Brace and World, Inc., 1962, p. 282.

economist is interested in the worth of his discipline for its own sake.

The social studies, on the other hand, consist mainly of the teachable portions of the social sciences, carefully selected and adapted for use in the schools. The over-arching purpose of the social studies is the development of desirable socio-civic behavior. As parts of the social studies, economics, history, and problems of American democracy are concerned with ethical considerations, ideals, and value judgments. "In the day-to-day work of the classroom, both the content and the method," Todd argues, "must contribute to the creation of desirable socio-economic behavior." Furthermore, efforts at revising the social studies that ignore this mandate are "doomed to endless frustration and certain failure." [2] The approach to economics as a social study must be basically psychological rather than strictly logical. While the social studies have an obligation to be accurate and reliable, and while they may at times use the inductive approach of inquiry and discovery, the aim is not the unearthing of new knowledge. No one expects a high school senior's critical essay on "A Comparison of Soviet and American Farm Problems" to be a contribution to human knowledge suitable for publication in *The American Economic Review*. In short, the social studies aspire to be no more than the social sciences simplified for pedagogical purposes.

In their zeal for analysis, model building, and structure, professional economists, learning theorists, and many others who pursue excellence through more rigorous training in scholarship on the high school level, tend to forget that, while economics teachers have an obligation to teach as much analysis as the traffic will bear, they must never lose sight of the horizons, the socioeconomic background, the interests, and the limitations of today's high school students. A student who does not understand grammar and logic will have difficulty in making a rational objective analysis of the arguments involved in fiscal policy.

Teaching Economic Understandings

In general, economic understandings can be introduced into the social studies curriculum in three major ways.

First, economic facts and concepts can be integrated with the content of the social studies and other subject areas by fusion and spiraling. Because the curriculum is already overcrowded, the integrated approach to economic education has considerable appeal. If basic economic concepts which constitute the foundation of our economic system can be fused with the existing curriculum, no new units of study deal-

[2] *Ibid.*, p. 290.

ing exclusively with economics need be added. Instead, the existing curriculum can be revised at all grade levels to incorporate appropriate economic concepts. By using the same basic concepts at all grade levels, economic understandings fused into a spiral curriculum can be deepened and enriched. The "degree of sophistication and complexity" should, of course, be altered at each grade level.[3] Furthermore, under this approach, the teacher is obligated to teach only the economic materials with which he is familiar. And, the student is made acquainted with economic thought, its application, and its implications, in small doses and in natural settings because economic institutions, principles, concepts, and analyses are dealt with as they arise in the study of history, government, business subjects, and home economics. Finally, because economic education permeates the entire K–12 curriculum, economic education becomes everybody's job.[4]

Second, economic education can be introduced as units on economics topics within such required courses as ninth grade World Geography, eleventh grade American history, and twelfth grade Problems of American Democracy. The proponents of this approach to economic education point out that not only can blocks of economics be included, but economic understanding will reach all secondary school students and at more than one grade level.

Third, economics can be taught as a separate subject, usually during one of the semesters of the senior year in high school. A systematic, well-organized economics course, taught by a teacher thoroughly grounded in economics and capitalizing on prior learnings, guarantees study in depth and develops competency in reasoning about economic principles and problems important to lifelong learning.[5]

In its study on the status of economics in the curriculum, the National Association of Secondary School Principals learned in 1965 that the principal issue among schoolmen was whether economic understanding is best achieved through scheduling separate economics courses or by incorporating economics instruction in other courses usually taken by most of the students.[6] The issue has been resolved in a sizable number of high schools by using both approaches. Among them are the high schools of New York City.

---

[3] John P. McIntyre and Joseph De Church, "The Development of a Total School Program in Economic Education," *Social Education*, 30:252 (April 1966).

[4] Norman W. Hauser, "Why, What and How of Economics in Secondary Schools of San Diego," *The Bulletin of the National Association of Secondary School Principals* (November 1965), pp. 139–140.

[5] Hauser, *op. cit.*, pp. 140–144.

[6] Galen Jones, "The Current Status of Economics Teaching in the High Schools of the United States," *The Bulletin of the National Association of Secondary School Principals* (November 1965), pp. 19–22.

The Professional Economist's View

As many professional economists see it, very little economics is actually being taught at any point in the public school curriculum at present, although an impressive array of economics topics is prescribed in various courses and units of study. Partly this is the result of fitting bits and pieces of economics into courses and units whose major purpose is not the teaching of essential information about the structure and operation of the American economy. Partly it is the result of failure to develop the topics sequentially and to treat them in terms of such underlying forces and processes as specialization and division of labor, competition, capital formation, and economic growth. In American history, for example, the development of the nation's transcontinental railroad network is usually presented as a dramatic conquest of nature with emphasis on miles of track, the airbrake, and the Pullman and the refrigerator car, rather than on the impact of the changes in transportation on specialization, division of labor, extent of the market, relative prices, industrial location, or employment opportunities. In short, professional economists deplore the descriptive approach to economic subject matter characterized by heavy emphasis upon matters of personal adjustment to the economy to the neglect of underlying processes, basic concepts, and the frame of reference necessary to recognize symptoms, understand causes, and evaluate issues. If problem-solving approaches are attempted, economists contend, facts and values are not separated, controversial issues are not faced, and only current manifestations of persistent problems are treated.

The Liberal Arts Approach

Professional economists usually advocate teaching economics in the liberal arts tradition. College textbooks, written by authorities like Paul A. Samuelson[7] and George Leland Bach,[8] emphasize structure. Economics is regarded as the study of the economy and its principles of order. As early as 1890, in his neoclassical *Principles of Economics,* Alfred Marshall suggested that economics provides an organon, that is, "an engine for the discovery of concrete truth." [9] Economists attempt to

[7] Paul A. Samuelson, *Economics: An Introductory Analysis,* 6th ed. New York, McGraw-Hill, 1964.

[8] George L. Bach, *Economics: An Introduction to Analysis and Policy,* 3rd ed. Englewood Cliffs, Prentice-Hall, 1960.

[9] Quoted by Laurence E. Leamer, *The Economist as Teacher: Informal Essays on the Collegiate Teaching of Economics,* Monograph C-13. Cincinnati, South-Western Publishing Company, 1965, p. 9.

discover regularities in choices and in economic activities from which they can deduce principles which are useful for offering explanations or for making predictions of economic behavior. The liberal arts approach to the teaching of economics predicates that the student be taught to understand models, that is, theoretical explanations of relationships among abstract variables, before he begins to identify these relationships in concrete situations.

Most social studies teachers are familiar with certain economic models. The following graph, showing the way in which supply and demand determine competitive market price, is an example of an economic model used by many teachers.

Let us assume that the following is true of the demand and supply of a certain type of ladies' shoes in the wholesale market. (Demand curve, DD; supply curve, SS.)

Number of pairs of shoes demanded at the price indicated	Assumed scale of prices (in dollars)	Number of pairs of shoes supplied at the price indicated
3,500	5	1,500
3,000	6	2,000
2,500	7	2,500
2,000	8	2,800
1,500	9	3,000
1,000	10	4,000

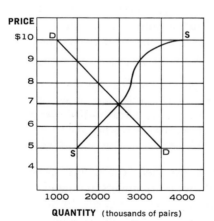

Under competitive conditions, the price for ladies' shoes in this particular wholesale market on that given day would be $7 (the intersection of the demand and the supply curves).

Structuring economics by the use of simplified models helps the high school student to see the economic world effectively, professional economists argue, because it provides an approach that enables the student to fit the pieces together and assimilate more of reality into his structural framework in his high school study of economics and later, when he has started his life's work. The analytical approach to the teaching of high school economics will be treated at length in Part II: Methods of Teaching the "New" Analytical Economics.

The Life-Adjustment Approach

The advocates of the life-adjustment approach to economic understanding disagree with the proponents of the liberal arts approach as to the kind of economic understanding that is most useful to high school students. As early as 1933, the need for a new approach to high school economics was so apparent that the United States Commissioner of Education appointed a National Committee on Economic Education made up of a dozen eminent educators and economists to explore the problem. In a memorandum based on the results of five years of work, the chairman, Dr. A. J. Stoddard, said in 1938 that instruction in economics, which was then largely limited to abstract theory, was "beyond the understanding of elementary and high school pupils." The setting was too remote and the viewpoint too far removed from the experience of the students. On the basis of the findings, the National Committee on Economic Education recommended "specifically an adoption of the consumer approach to the study of economics."

G. Derwood Baker, a pioneer in the economic-education movement, said,

How to get a job, how to budget income, how to use credit, labor-management relations, social security, farm price supports, the role of profits in our economy, the hazards of inflation—these are some of the topics that affect and puzzle the teenager, the teacher, the farmer, and the banker. They are typical of the problems which must be dealt with in the school.

Knowledge which can help consumers spend their money more wisely eventually draws on an understanding of economic forces which influence prices and production policies. In the late 1960's, some high school teachers still believe that an economics course which stresses consumer education is the most practical course for below-average students. The personal-problems approach is a powerful motivational force. It appeals to teen-agers, who have average annual per capita incomes of $300, much of which is used for discretionary spending.

The Citizenship-Education Approach

Some schoolmen argue that economics should be considered a part of citizenship education and that all social studies areas should contribute to a growing understanding of persistent economic issues in our society. Although education for citizenship is an aim of both the liberal arts and the life-adjustment approach, the proponents of economics for citizenship do not believe that emphasis on analysis or a personalized approach is necessary, for example, to an understanding of the menace of monopolies to the general welfare or of the proper role of the government in a mixed economy such as ours. The citizenship-education approach stresses institutions and the skills of critical thinking rather than models and other analytical tools. Some feel that no models are necessary, for example, to follow and understand debates over issues which are carried on in Congress, the state legislature, or the local community. Moreover, by focusing on contemporary economic problems, the proponents of economics for citizenship hope to create a lifelong interest in economic controversies and in public policy.

The Challenge of Analytical Economics

The professional economist has posed a fresh challenge to the schools by his insistence on conceptual content instead of information and on analysis in place of description as a method of teaching. Can teachers teach concepts, models, and analysis to a large percentage of the students? If not, should the schools offer economics only for those students who can learn at a certain level of abstraction? An experienced, well-trained teacher of high school economics will argue that an analytical approach can and should be used for both the college-bound and the terminal student—but not exclusively. Analysis and a few models are indispensable, he contends, but all theory must be convincingly related to a world the student recognizes. It is unrealistic to expect all students to apply even simple economic models and simple abstractions successfully to a complex economic world. The other social sciences do not make similar demands. Where worldly applications are asked of students, as in sociology or political science, the subject matter is more descriptive, less analytical, and probably easier to relate to personal experience.

An Eclectic Approach

In teaching some topics, such as comparative economic systems, the approach should be chiefly analytical. In teaching others, such as the role of the consumer in a free-enterprise economy, the approach must, of necessity, be more descriptive, personalized, and institutional. The job of the high school teacher is to teach the economic ABC's to all students, to raise their functional literacy in the subject, and to encourage good economic citizenship on their part. If, in the process, he can take some of his students farther along the road to economic understanding, a teacher will not shirk his responsibility.

PART II

Methods of Teaching the "New" Analytical Economics

> The most important step toward understanding in economics—as in other branches of knowledge—is the replacement of emotional, unreasoned judgments by objective, rational analysis.
>
> *The Task Force Report*

4 *The High School Economics Class: The Students and the Teacher*

The High School Senior

Economics is usually taught as a one-semester course in the twelfth year to high school seniors. All high school seniors belong to some sort of teenage society with its own culture and demands. It may be part of a wealthy suburban community or a deprived segment of our population dwelling in the ghettos of a great city, in the gray areas of small towns, or in the hollows of Appalachia. As an economics teacher, you are teaching individuals who are a persuasive and potent force influencing consumer spending today. The twenty-five million teenagers in our affluent and child-oriented society constitute a special market in themselves with $10 to $15 billion in buying power, much of which is discretionary. In fact, the disposable income of $300 which the average American teenager enjoys is larger than the average industrial income of two thirds of the world's adult population. While two thirds of the teenager's income comes from allowances, one third comes from part-time jobs. *The students sitting before you are already an important part of our economy: they have a reservoir of economic experience upon which you, as an alert teacher, can draw.*

Physically, emotionally, and intellectually, the high school senior is more akin to the college freshman than to the younger adolescent. His attention span is longer—long enough, in fact, to profit from an occasional lecture. He is more stable, more secure, more adult. Yet he has not completely cast off his moorings to adolescence. The understanding economics teacher, therefore, can still use the motivating drives of the developmental tasks of youth first described by Robert J. Havighurst a quarter of a century ago.

The Developmental Tasks of Youth

The developmental tasks of youth are the learnings or adjustments which are necessary to create a well-rounded, mature adult. The major tasks include:

1. *Coming to terms with one's own body,* that is, worries over physical appearance, size, manliness, or feminine beauty. This drive can be tapped when one is teaching the economic role of the teenager in the American economy and consumers' problems in general.

2. *Learning new relationships to one's age mates,* that is, the need for acceptance by the peer group, the painful desire to conform (which involves the right behavior, the right clothes, the right crowd, and interest in the opposite sex). This drive can be used in discussing hidden persuaders, artificial obsolescence, and advertising in general.

3. *Achieving independence from one's parents.* The teacher can capitalize on this drive in teaching labor, the need for salable skills, the achievement of financial independence, and the economic value of a good education in general.

4. *Achieving adult and economic status.* This task involves symbols like excessive make-up, freakish dress, staying out late, and the right to use the family car. The status drive is part of the foundation of the entire economics course, that is, to develop young men and women competent in both economic and political spheres.

5. *Acquiring self-confidence and a system of values.* The yearnings on the part of the adolescent for the good are real. Idealism can be stressed in teaching the goals of the good economic society and it can undergird policy judgments during the entire course.

Regardless of what teachers want, the developmental tasks of youth are the primary interest of students of junior and senior high school age. References to the trials and tribulations of newlyweds, the reasons that girls rarely marry below their standards of living, and status symbols, such as one's own car, arouse immediate interest.

The High School Teacher

The knowledgeable teacher understands the developmental tasks of his students and utilizes these dynamic drives to motivate his teaching.

1. *A good economics teacher understands and respects his students.*

Respecting one's students means being courteous, considerate, friendly, and treating all of them alike without favor or prejudice. Understanding involves empathy, a saving sense of humor, and an in-depth knowledge of the characteristics of adolescents and the problems of youth. In short, the teacher sets an example of a mature, tolerant, understanding adult—a friend, a guide, a resource person, but not the pupil's pal.

2. *A good economics teacher respects the subject he teaches.* He makes economics come alive by his enthusiasm which is contagious and by his understanding of the heart of the problem which makes for clarity. He is ready and able, when occasion demands, to move away from his textbook and his lesson plan for the day to seek wider horizons. He feels that the textbook is a useful aid but he does not let it dominate his teaching.

3. *A good economics teacher is convinced that learning is an active process.* He knows that a hunter cannot take unwilling dogs on a hunt. His lesson plans provide ample opportunity for pupil activity. He feels that pupils must have a vital part in discovering a generalization, in phrasing it, and in applying it.

4. *A good economics teacher knows that first-hand experiences must precede generalizations.* A single visual aid often supplies the stimulation of thousands of words. Verbalisms, textbook phraseology, and pat expressions are avoided. Pupils are encouraged to say things in their own words and to furnish examples based on their own daily experiences. He makes assignments that touch the students' real interests, that is, on their developmental goals. Such assignments are self-motivating.

5. *A good economics teacher strives to relate learning activities to students' needs.* He suggests to his boys and girls experiences that may clarify the goals they are seeking through reading (especially biography), through participation in debating societies and economics clubs, and through individual investigations and reports. He uses down-to-earth examples and always begins with the students' thinking on topics such as communism, the war on poverty, and union activities, rather than with the scholarship of the subject.

6. *A good economics teacher arranges learning activities, especially skills, in graded sequence.* He understands that even in a subject like economics, which stresses analysis and logic, the psychological approach is the most effective. He touches only one difficulty at a time. His questions follow a psychological sequence. He gives his students time to engage in decision-making, to weigh evidence, and to criticize. He knows that students must grow in attitudes and skills as well as in understandings. Each lesson, therefore, is pointed toward a definite goal that is as clear to the students as it is to the teacher.

Criteria for Self-Evaluation

The two checklists that follow are designed to offer criteria for self-evaluation in two important aspects of the individual's life as a teacher.

CHECKLIST FOR SELF-EVALUATION: PERSONAL APPEARANCE, SPEECH, AND MANNERISMS

I. *Personal Appearance*
1. Are you always neat, poised, and well-groomed?
2. Are your clothes in good taste for the time, the place, the occasion, and your age?
3. Do you avoid extremes in styles, hair-dos, and personal adornment?
4. Is your posture good?

II. *Speech*
1. Is your voice calm? low? modulated? distinct?
2. Are you clearly heard by all students in the room?
3. Do you speak too fast? too slowly? gruffly? in a drawl? with a lisp?
4. Do you pronounce words correctly? enunciate carefully?
5. Do you avoid slang? street language? uncultured speech?

III. *Mannerisms*
1. Do you repeatedly use expressions such as "Good," "Now boys and girls," and "Class, what do you think?"
2. Are you a compulsive talker?
3. Do you make nervous gestures? frequently hesitate? repeat questions and answers?

CHECKLIST FOR SELF-APPRAISAL: TEACHER-PUPIL RAPPORT
1. Do you understand the implications of "the developmental tasks of youth"?
2. Do your students share your enthusiasm for economics? Do you involve them in the lesson? Do they capture some of the excitement that is economics?
3. Do your students respect your scholarship? your judgment? your sense of values?
4. Are your students interested in their work? eager to participate? quick to respond?
5. Do your students look to you as a leader? as a resource person? for guidance?
6. Do your students feel free to express their views without fear of reprisal?

7. Is your manner pleasant but firm?
8. Do you try to curry favor with your students by being "easy"? "a pal"? "one of the boys"?

Teaching the Language of Economics

The economics teacher has two special tasks to perform which relate to the nature of his subject. The first is teaching the language of the economist. The terminology of economics is one of the things that bother the beginner in economics most.

Beginning teachers of economics, like some professional economists, often make unwarranted assumptions regarding the educational and experiential background that students need for effective economic understanding. An understanding of the vocabulary of economics is extremely important. It is very difficult to think rationally or to talk intelligently about any subject without some knowledge of the special vocabulary. This is especially true of the language of professional economists. When teachers use words commonly employed in mass media, they cannot assume that high school students have mastered either their meanings or their implications. Teachers must constantly ask themselves: Do my students know the meaning of *productivity, free enterprise, social insurance, communism, economic growth, inflation, recession, deficit financing,* and *capital formation* or *capital depreciation?* Furthermore, economists may use words in common usage which have specialized meanings in economics. For example, the layman refers to the purchase of shares of stocks and bonds and the purchase of real estate as "investment," but, to the economist, "investment" is used in a special sense. It refers to the process of capital formation, that is, to the accumulation of buildings, machinery, highways, and the like. In the terminology of economics, "land," as a factor of production, includes all natural resources, not just the earth's surface. "Value" means the power of a good to command another in return for it, not just usefulness. And, in "economicese," "scarcity" refers only to the need to make choices in the allocation of material resources, not poverty or insufficiency, as it does in laymen's language. The student must also learn to distinguish between a host of look-alikes: "standard of living" and "cost of living"; "balance of trade" and "balance of payments"; "tax base" and "tax rate"; "economic growth" and "economic development"; and so on.

Combating Economic Folklore and Mythology

The second special task of the economics teacher is combating economic folklore and economic mythology. Before the high school teacher can introduce the student to the formal study of economics, he must clear away much of the economic folklore which students bring to class with them. John Kenneth Galbraith has called this folklore, which he describes so lucidly for us in *The Affluent Society*, "the conventional wisdom." The conventional wisdom is the system of values and beliefs at any given time in history to which everyone is expected to subscribe, and which is carefully and purposefully protected from contamination by critical analysis. Calvin Coolidge's remark that we need "less government in business and more business in government" is one such unexamined assumption. Another illustration is the belief that the federal budget, like the household budget, should always be balanced. High school students believe many things about economics that are not true. In no other subject do students have so many ideas and fixed opinions about what they are studying as in economics. Furthermore, they feel perfectly competent to advise, criticize, judge, and even abuse professionals. Indeed, the high school economics teacher soon discovers that "a little knowledge is worse than none" in his chosen field.

The Teacher and Class in Action

The First Day in Economics

In many respects, your first meeting with your first economics class is a crucial one. Naturally, your new students want to know what you are like, and, whether economics will be "hard" or "easy." In short, both your course and you are going to be sized up. If you enter your economics classroom as if you belonged there, expecting no difficulties and intending to stand for no nonsense, you will be making a good first impression. You must appear to know exactly what you expect to do and what you expect of the class. The secret, of course, is *really* knowing what you want to do because you have planned every activity in advance and anticipated every foreseeable difficulty. Careful planning will relieve you of that lost feeling. If you appear calm and confident (even though you really may not be), the class will sense that you mean business. Remember: students respect competence and strength, not indecision and weakness.

The following suggestions will help you in organizing the first day's work with a minimum of effort and with maximum effect.

1. Go to your room *before* your class arrives. It is better psychologically for you to welcome the class than for the class to welcome you. Furthermore, your presence in the room from the very beginning will inhibit any possible tendencies toward disorder or confusion.

2. Write your name clearly on the front board where all the students can see it.

3. Begin the class promptly by having the students fill out attendance cards or a simple questionnaire. If the students are immediately caught up in the business at hand, they cannot organize for fun and frolic. Request students who gravitate to the rear of the room to change to seats in the front. Do this firmly but gently. In seating students, separate those who greet each other as long-lost brothers. Break up this happy reunion despite pleadings, excuses, or threats.

4. Seat at the front of the room students who have difficulty seeing or hearing.

5. Some teachers devote the remainder of the period to having the pupils take notes on an outline of the semester's work and their requirements in the matter of readings, reports, and homework. Others use the first lesson to introduce economics vividly by discussion and lecturette (see below, *A Theme for the Economics Course*), deferring to the second session of the class the important task of setting forth class requirements.

6. Make it emphatically clear from the very start that the dismissal bell is a signal for *you* and not for the students. The members of the class are not to rise and head for the door until *you* dismiss them. The class must understand that it does not dismiss itself or you.

A Theme for the Economics Course

Economics teachers often use a major course theme to unify and sharpen interest in their subject. The role of the teenager in the American economy is such a theme. The Pittsburgh Public Schools have focused on comparative economic systems as the theme for their ninth graders. The author has successfully used a problem—How much liberty are you willing to surrender for economic security?—as the recurrent theme in his classes. This is a question which comes into sharp focus whenever the class discusses our dual or mixed economy, government ownership, regulation and control, comparative economic systems, and the like. William Freund, an economist, has suggested that economics on the high school level can be taught by focusing the course on the Great Depression of 1929 and by relating specific topics to the causes, consequences, and changes which the Great Depression effected in the relationship of government to business as exemplified by the Employment Act of 1946, and by the thinking on the role of government in economic affairs by professional economists and the American public. Certainly our fear of mass post-war unemployment in the late 1940's, our worries about the rate of economic growth in the United States as compared with the Russian, the Japanese, and the West German in the 1950's, and our concern about our islands of poverty in a sea of affluence in the 1960's stem from the Great Depression of 1929.

The value of having a course theme or focus of attention is undeniable. The first class session is the best time to set your course theme squarely, vividly, and forthrightly before your class.

Classroom Discipline

Discipline has never been a major problem of the economics teacher largely because the course is usually taught by experienced teachers to seniors. Troublemakers have dropped out in lower terms and economics is generally still an elective subject chosen by, not foisted on, the students. Yet there is scarcely a teacher who has not at some time or other encountered discipline problems even among seniors.

There is, of course, no royal road or easy way to achieving good discipline. While the teacher's personality plays a part, it is not a case of "either you have it or you don't." Good discipline arises out of orderly procedures and purposeful meaningful activities. The astute teacher establishes a set of simple, readily understood, and easily enforced routines that habituate the student to orderly procedures and eliminate foci of disorder. Among the routines are the following.

1. Taking attendance (by using a seating chart, not a roll call)
2. Collecting and distributing papers and materials
3. Checking homework
4. Entering and leaving the room
5. Using the pass
6. Enforcing school rules regarding lateness and absence from class

The following general suggestions may prove useful in dealing with incipient discipline problems.

1. Try to handle your own problems. In general, do not refer a pupil to a higher authority until you have exhausted the means at your own disposal for dealing with him.

2. Suggest to the errant student that you and he "reason together." A heart-to-heart talk often succeeds better than throwing the book at him.

3. Consider the intent of the offender before arriving at your verdict.

4. If punishment is necessary, let it be certain and swift.

5. Handle discipline problems in private. It avoids making a hero of the culprit and enables both parties to save face.

6. Change seats of troublemakers.

7. Spot potential offenders early and deal firmly with them.

8. Move about the room freely. Often standing in the vicinity of a potential trouble spot has a salutary effect.

9. Keep the class occupied. The devil finds work for idle hands.

10. There is no substitute for an interesting, worthwhile, well-planned lesson. Students who are interested in a lesson, who are participating enthusiastically, and who feel that they are learning, will not misbehave.

If discipline is not your strongest point, use the following checklist. It may pinpoint your difficulty.

CHECKLIST FOR SELF-EVALUATION: MAINTAINING GOOD CLASSROOM DISCIPLINE

1. Are you always well-prepared?

2. Do you start your lessons promptly?

3. Do you have well-established class routines?

4. Do you motivate each lesson?

5. Do your students understand the aim of each lesson, accept it as worthwhile, and share in its formulation?

6. Do you vary your lessons, your methods, and your approach?

7. Are your vocabulary and the content of your lesson within the comprehension of the class?

8. Do you permit the calling out of answers? chorus answers? wisecracks?

9. Do you dismiss your class at the end of the period, or does the bell do it for you?

10. Do you give regular, motivated, worthwhile homework assignments?

11. Do you give frequent tests and oral quizzes? check homework and notebooks? and generally keep your students posted on their progress?

12. Do you permit inattentive students to whisper while the floor is held by another student or you?

13. Do you treat everyone alike, or do you have pets?

14. Do you have a tendency to make a federal case out of a misdemeanor?

15. Do your students accept you as an example of a mature, understanding adult?

5   Aims and Objectives

Major Goals of an Economics Course for Our Time

Alfred Marshall, the great neoclassical economist, once observed that the aim of economics should be to produce citizens "with cool heads and warm hearts" who would be able and willing to use their knowledge "to open up to all the material means of a refined and noble life." Every schoolman knows that, properly taught, economics can make worthy contributions to the education of students of high school age. It can acquaint the students with the economic institutions that are so much a part of their daily lives. It can acquaint them with a way of thinking about economic issues that will replace careless, emotional thinking with logical, rational analysis. And, finally, it can impart an understanding of the many complicated and vexing economic and social problems that confront the American people and give the students the tools with which to analyze critically and choose wisely from among proposed policies.

What should be the characteristics of a one-semester twelfth-grade high school economics course, based on these general principles and geared to the demands of our time?

First, it should be a realistic course which attempts to create a life-long interest in real-world economic problems. It should foster economic understanding for citizenship in the sense in which the National Task Force uses the term, that is, it should attempt to provide a meaningful introduction to the economic process—to concepts, facts, and principles that a person needs in order to function responsibly as a citizen and decision-maker in a democratic private-enterprise economy.

Second, it should present an overview of our economic system, its institutions, and its problems. Ideally, it should be a course which could be called "An Introduction to Economic Study" rather than a "Principles" or a Survey course. While the basic structure of the discipline should be emphasized throughout the course, it would of necessity also describe economic institutions because, before a person can think analytically about, let us say, the farm problem as it exists in the United States and in the Soviet Union, he must know the facts. And, in the process, he must unlearn a great deal of economic mythology and economic folklore.

Third, the course should develop a way of thinking about economic problems. It should provide an orientation to economics by introducing the student to fundamental problems, basic forces at work in the economy, and key concepts and principles, all of which help to organize his thinking about the economic process.

Fourth, it should provide a preview of the scope and the methods of economics in the light of which subsequent courses take on added meaning. In short, it should develop models which would serve as tools for continuing economic analysis. During the 1950's, concern for economic growth was the great obsession. Today the stress is on the amelioration of poverty. But, with basic economic tools in his possession, the high school student of today will be equipped to understand the issues which become current in the 1970's and 1980's.

Fifth, the economics course of the late 1960's should not shy away from current controversial issues. It should try to capture "some of the excitement that is economics," that is, "a sense of unresolved issues, of freemen grappling with choices that involve trade-offs—a little more success in achieving full employment coming perhaps at the expense of a little less success in maintaining stable prices." [1] It would nurture in high school students, within their capacities, skill in the use of economic analysis to explore issues such as those surrounding medicare, the negative income tax, collective bargaining, and public spending, which make economics so perplexing, so fascinating, and so infuriating to many people.

Sixth, the economics course of our time should be a selective course. It should present evidence of the courage to exclude as well as the imagination to include. Elementary textbooks in economics, seeking to incorporate new developments and to keep up with graduate instruction, tend to become abridged encyclopedias. While Professor Coleman discovered no single way to be most effective in teaching economics, he set up certain direction signs. Teach less, but teach in greater depth. Emphasize the ties between economics and the various social studies. Stress critical thinking with the use of raw statistical data and sources which provide "evidence." And, develop and use new materials in greater abundance. [2]

[1] John R. Coleman, "Second Thoughts on Economics in the Schools," *Social Education*, 30:77 (February 1965).
[2] "Council Reports," *Joint Council on Economic Education Newsletter* (May 1964), p. 8.

Understandings

The goals described above constitute the overall objectives of an economics course for the late 1960's. An objective has been defined as "a specific goal, useful in life," to be achieved by a unit, an entire lesson, or a part of a lesson. In planning specific daily lessons, teachers should of course keep in mind specific objectives such as understandings, attitudes, and skills.

Understandings is the term used by teachers for conceptual learning. Economics teachers are vitally concerned with the development of concepts, generalizations, and principles, which constitute the basic structure of the discipline. Conceptual learning, of course, must be based on a body of carefully selected pertinent facts. At present, economics, as a discipline, is probably able to conceptualize its theoretical framework (or structure) more effectively than the other high school social studies. In planning daily lessons, teachers should keep in mind specific understandings such as the following.

1. Sufficient information regarding the economic world in which we live to lay the foundation for the replacement of emotional judgment by objective, rational analysis

2. An understanding of the economic institutions in the United States, how they came about, and how they operate

3. A deepened understanding of American political, social, and economic institutions in comparison and contrast with those of other nations

4. Sufficient command of the methodology of the discipline and sufficient knowledge of its structure to arrive at valid conclusions on the basis of economic analysis

Attitudes

Attitudes relate to values, appreciations, and ideals that social studies teachers seek to instill in the learner. Among the attitudes that the economics teacher may wish to instill are:

1. A commitment to well-informed, alert, and responsible citizenship such as carrying out tax obligations of every kind and voting on state and national issues of economic import

2. An interest in, and concern for, the social, political, and economic problems created by the technological developments of the past century

Skills

Skills include ways of dealing with economics as a field of study and with people in human association. Among the general social-studies skills which high school economics teachers stress are:

1. *Work-Study Skills:* reading, outlining, interpretation of graphs, charts, and tables, and statistical analysis

2. *Thinking Skills:* critical thinking and problem solving

3. *Group-Process Skills:* leading and participating in group under-takings such as visits to industrial and commercial enterprises, surveys, interviews, and panels

4. *Living Skills:* acting responsibly and cooperating with one's group.

Specifically, the economics teacher should stress:

1. Information and skill sufficient to perform efficiently and wisely such functions as reading with comprehension the more thoughtful parts of newspapers and magazines.

2. Information and skill sufficient to perform efficiently and wisely the actions usually associated with good economic citizenship such as analyzing issues, making wise choices, and using basic problem-solving techniques. In the process, the student should become aware of such common blocks to critical thinking as: 1) failure to define terms, 2) faulty comparisons (the federal budget with a household budget), 3) hasty generalizations, 4) the abuse of statistics, and 5) propaganda tricks (glittering generalities, transfer, testimonials, plain folks, card stacking, and the band wagon).

3. Interpretation of material presented in graphic form such as charts, tables, and diagrams. In the process, the student should learn 1) to identify central issues, 2) to recognize underlying assumptions, 3) to evaluate evidence or authority (detecting bias, stereotypes, inconsistencies, irrelevant and unverifiable data) and, 4) to draw warranted conclusions.

Relationship of Purpose to Method

No single method of teaching is good for all economic topics, at all times, in all schools, and for all students. There is a close relationship, however, between purpose and method in teaching economics. Teachers should stress objectives and concepts in planning their daily lessons because a teacher who has a clear understanding of his purpose or aim can accomplish more than one who blindly follows the book or the new syllabus. By reflection, analysis, and living through the lesson for the next day, an economics teacher can devise a systematic and effective lesson plan for reaching his goal. For example, if he is teaching an over-view of a new topic in the unit on Money and Banking, such as the Federal Reserve System, he can often do this best by exhibiting a film-strip or having his class view a sound film on the subject. Some topics, such as the regulation of public utilities, lend themselves to case studies. Others, such as the difficulties encountered by a developing nation, should be tackled by problem-solving techniques. In short, purpose, in most cases, determines method.

6 *Planning the Economics Lesson*

Planning Your Work

Over two thousand years ago, Socrates used inquiry and discovery techniques while Aristotle taught through lectures and seminars. More recently, Mr. Chips conducted old-fashioned recitations that are frowned upon today. Yet, despite diversity in method, all were successful teachers, respected and admired by their devoted students. There is no one guaranteed method that can make a person a good teacher. A method is simply a procedure which involves a series of teacher-directed activities designed to stimulate student learning.

Why study methods? Because with methods appropriate to the understandings or concepts to be taught, a teacher can accomplish more if he has a clear understanding of his purpose or objectives than if he proceeds in a random ad hoc manner. Using a particular method usually forces a teacher to think through his procedures, a process which, in itself, helps him to become orderly and systematic in teaching his students. Finally, methods provide patterns for teaching. Some patterns may be better suited for teaching opportunity costs than for teaching comparative economic systems.

One thing is certain: Without systematic, thorough planning the beginning teacher will never attain competence in teaching economics. While it may be true that a few born teachers are able to conjure a good economics lesson out of thin air, little effective and genuinely useful classroom teaching can be accomplished by this sort of legerdemain. Seasoned teachers, who have a rich and varied experience upon which to draw, do not have to plan their lessons in as great detail as does the beginner, but all teachers who approach their tasks honestly and conscientiously, feel the need of knowing exactly what they intend to do and how they plan to do it. Charm, erudition, inspiration, humor, rapport, and experience are no substitutes for the consistent and effective planning of instruction.

All good planning has common elements. In general, economics lesson plans should include economic understandings, objectives involving the reenforcement of skills and attitudes, detailed procedures for teaching the lesson and pivotal (or key) questions to be asked in order to stimulate class discussion. Wherever it is possible to do so, the aim of the lesson should be stated as a problem and emphasis placed on inductive reasoning. Teachers should be careful not to overload their lessons, that is, introduce too many or too complicated ideas. As John Locke once noted, "The great art of learning is to understand a little at a time."

In planning his lessons, a teacher must always keep in mind the aims and objectives of his course and the laws of learning. He must see the way in which the small job he is doing on a particular day fits into the larger unit of which it is a part. Only thus can he make lucid the logic and pertinence of the daily classroom activities to the students. A knowledgeable teacher utilizes group processes and student involvement. He reenforces skills such as critical thinking and suspended judgment. And, above all, he hopes to achieve effects which will outlast the hour devoted to the topic of the day.

Long- and Short-Range Planning

Economics is not a subject that can be effectively taught by reading a high school textbook or keeping a chapter ahead of the class. It is a challenge even to experienced teachers to impart real understanding of economic concepts and the basic structure of the discipline to students. Just as a mathematics or a physics teacher must be schooled in his subject, so must the high school teacher of economics be educated in basic economics regardless of his skill in history, his personal charm, or his good intentions.

Economics teachers engage in both long-range and short-range planning of their courses. If you are assigned to teach economics during the coming semester, ask for the following materials:

1. The official state or city syllabus or course of study in economics
2. The teacher's guide or prospectus for economics, drawn up by the department
3. Mimeographed uniform assignment sheets for economics
4. The textbook for the course.

If a copy of the textbook is the only thing available, consult *Economic Education in the Schools,* the Report of the National Task Force. It contains helpful hints regarding both the methodology and the content of a good analytical one-semester high school course.

If you are to begin teaching economics, take ample time to become familiar with the materials and to engage in long-range planning. Familiarity with the scope and sequence of the course and the teaching materials inspires confidence. Nothing makes a teacher feel so insecure as being only one or two lessons ahead of the class. It is also helpful to do the following:

1. Using the term calendar, or any similar device you may wish to employ, calculate the actual amount of time you have for classroom instruction. Make due allowance for review, examinations, school excursions, and snow days. You can generally count on 16 weeks of solid instruction each semester.

2. Consult your syllabi and determine the amount of time to spend on the various units, topics, and sub-topics. Of necessity, this plan will have to be flexible, but you will at least begin your work knowing approximately what you are going to do and how long it will take you. You will know where you are going and why. You may have to alter your course here and there as circumstances demand, but you will know your destination.

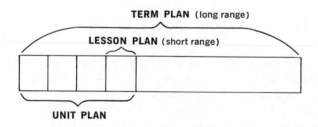

Short-range planning consists of preparing a series of lessons in a unit such as Labor Problems or Comparative Economic Systems. A unit is a series of related experiences organized around a central problem, theme, or topic of student interest or concern. One advantage of planning a unit in advance is that doing so compels the teacher to select relevant materials with discrimination, to plot his course in detail, and to set up a timetable for reaching his destination. Perhaps the most familiar aspect of short-range planning is making a daily lesson plan.

Lesson Plans

Authorities agree that a good lesson plan helps the teacher to improve both his classroom management and his instruction. A good lesson plan insures forethought, freshness of preparation, clarification of aims, and rigid selection of materials and contributes to the achievement of one's objectives. It guarantees orderly procedure, attention to points for emphasis, better timing, the availability of supplementary materials, and the inclusion of key questions for consideration by the class. Moreover, because it is conducive to confidence, a good lesson plan frees the teacher's mind for further inventiveness, and results in better teaching. As a consequence, better behavior, more active participation, and improved effort on the part of the students ensue.

A good lesson plan should include the following elements common to all good teaching.

1. *Definite, worthwhile aims.* The aims should be lucidly stated in terms of the understandings, skills, and attitudes you expect the students to achieve during the class period.

2. *Motivation to arouse immediate interest.* Will you start with a provocative question? a problem? an amusing cartoon? a link with their past experiences? an anecdote? a current event? Indicate in your lesson plan just what you expect to do to stimulate students to anticipate the lesson that is to follow.

3. *Stimulating procedures.* How do you plan to achieve your objectives? Indicate broadly the teaching techniques and pupil activities you expect to use as well as the general direction you expect your lesson to take.

4. *Development by questioning or other pivotal device, such as an audio-visual aid.* Unless the recitation pattern takes the form of a panel, forum, roundtable, or committee reports, indicate the large, thought-provoking (pivotal) questions around which the lesson will revolve. Such questions should be logical, sequential, and personal-experience-oriented, if possible.

5. *Illustrative material.* Indicate the pictures, duplicated materials, maps, transparencies, audio-visual aids, if any, you will use during the lesson.

6. *Medial and final summaries and application.* Provide time *during* the course of the lesson to clinch important arguments and points by means of *medial* summaries and at the end of the lesson for a *final* summary. Test pupils' grasp of the concepts, understandings, and skills by providing for applications to a current problem of interest or concern to the students. Indicate the pivotal question or closing activity through which you intend to clinch the main ideas.

A purposeful, clear, definite assignment for the following day. The student's approach to the subject, his mental set, his response in the next class session are all determined by the manner in which the assignment is made. The kind and amount of study, the carry-over values, the attitudes acquired during study, the study problem itself, all are inextricably involved in the assignment.

Model Lesson Plan

The lesson plan which follows is designed primarily to illustrate the various elements common to all good teaching described above. Each part of the plan is labeled in CAPITAL LETTERS, i.e., AIMS, MOTIVATION, SUMMARY. Explanatory notes, introduced to clarify certain aspects of the plan but not a part of the lesson per se, are bracketed. The model plan was drawn up for the first of two lessons on profits, "The Role of Profits in a Market System," in *The Modern Economy in Action: An Analytical Approach* by Alexander, Prehn, and Sametz. It is assumed that the assignment for the day is based on the "Questions for Review." In preparing their answers, the students read pp. 202–206. As an alternative, the teacher might have assigned pertinent questions on profits in Walter Harris' Workbook which accompanies *The Modern Economy in Action.* The end-of-chapter questions follow:

ASSIGNMENT: "Questions for Review"
1. Profits mean different things to different people.
    (a) What are profits?
    (b) Why is it important to differentiate between the several meanings of profits?
    (c) Why do economists call profits a residual return?
2. Explain briefly two ways in which profits may be measured.
3. (a) What is meant by an incentive?
    (b) Mention the chief ways in which profits serve as an incentive in our competitive economy.
    (c) Do all economic systems use profits as an incentive? Explain your answer.
4. Why do accountants draw up a profit and loss statement?

The assignment at the end of the model lesson plan is designed to prepare the class for the next day's lesson, "Why does the health of the American economy depend on profits?" Although both lessons draw upon the content of the chapter on profits in *The Modern Economy in*

Action, the teacher in his lesson plan departs freely at times from the text. Such departures, if they are logical and germane to the lesson, add interest and zest, challenge the student to use his critical and analytical powers, and appeal to his imagination. (Another detailed lesson plan appears at the end of Chapter 8, "Economic Analysis Through Developmental-Discussion Techniques.")

TOPIC: Why do profits play a vital role in a free-enterprise economy? [If possible, the topic, or the aim of a lesson, should be posed as a problem and phrased as a question.]

AIMS

1. To understand how the profit incentive stimulates entrepreneurs to risk losses in the hope of reaping profits. [Note how the aim serves as a common thread from the motivation to the final summary.]

2. To encourage students to view the realities of the business world rationally, realistically, and analytically. [A good lesson plan provides for the development of attitudes and skills as well as understandings.]

MOTIVATION: [The motivation serves as a springboard to the lesson. It sets the tone, arouses curiosity, aids in the formulation of the aim, and personalizes the lesson.]

A TRUE STORY

Jacqueline Jacquard was jubilant. Her accountant had told her that very afternoon, that at the end of her first year as a milliner, she had cleared $8,000 in her own little shop on Main Street. To celebrate her success, she invited her fiancé, Charles Michaud, a college economist, to dinner. Miss Jacquard was crestfallen when Professor Michaud told her, as tactfully as he could, that she had not made a profit. In fact, she was probably operating at a loss! Who do you think was correct? Why? [Student discussion, based on the assignment in *The Modern Economy in Action*, will bring out the difference between the accountant's and the economist's view as to what constitutes profits. The crucial point, of course, is the role of wages of management. If Miss Jacquard can earn $10,000 managing someone else's millinery shop, she is indeed losing $2,000 a year!]

Content Outline	*Pivotal Questions*
[Use the chalkboard for illustrations to present the distinction between the accountant's and the economist's view of profits, which the story elicits.]	How do the views of the accountant and those of the economist differ regarding the nature of profits?
Definitions of Profits	
Accountant's View	
Total Income	
−Applicable expenses	
Profits	
Economist's View	
Total Income	
−All explicit expenses and wages of management, rent on land owned, and interest on capital invested by the entrepreneur	
Pure profits	
Profit incentive is the motivating force in a free-enterprise economy.	Why do ambitious young people like Jacqueline Jacquard go into business for themselves?
	Why may Miss Jacquard decide to stay in business even if she is not receiving profits at present?
Rewards for Entrepreneurship	
1. Profits, immediate or future	
2. Status in community	
3. Own boss, etc.	
The profit incentive induces entrepreneurs to	What did Adam Smith, "the father of modern economics," mean when he said that each businessman is led as if by an invisible hand to produce the goods and services society needs?
1. Assume risks	
2. Organize and manage the business	
3. Advertise product, etc.	
And to produce goods and services, usually under competitive conditions, at prices which consumers can afford to pay.	
Profits—a residual return, the remains after all other factors,	*MEDIAL SUMMARY* Why have profits been com-

Content Outline	*Pivotal Questions*
including wages of management, have been paid.	pared to a residue that remains in a test tube after a chemical reaction has taken place?
Causes of Profits [List on chalkboard for emphasis.] 1. Successful innovation 2. Return for assumption of risk 3. Varying degrees of monopoly power 4. Windfall	Why do some businesses make money even though the management may be careless and inefficient while other businesses, run by efficient, hardworking managers, fail?
Causes for Business Failures 1. Poor management and neglect 2. Insufficient volume of sales 3. Inexperience 4. Lack of capital 5. Granting of too much credit 6. Wrong location for business	Each day a thousand new businesses are born and a thousand other businesses die. Why do some businesses fail?
[Review of salient points in entire lesson.]	*SUMMARY* Why do some economists refer to the American economy as a "profit and loss" economy?
Characteristics Essential to Business Success 1. Initiative and hard work 2. Friendliness and interest in people 3. Sense of responsibility 4. Leadership 5. Executive ability	*APPLICATION* What questions would you ask yourself before you decided to open a business of your own?

ASSIGNMENT (for the next lesson): Why does the health of a free-enterprise economy depend upon profits? Have the students read pp. 206–210, in *The Modern Economy in Action.* (Questions are numbered as they appear in "Questions for Review.") [Some teachers may prefer to make the assignment to the *Workbook.* "Discussion Questions" in the text are probably most useful for the enrichment of the lesson proper. If the class has the requisite ability and interest, the teacher may also assign a reading or an activity.]

ASSIGNMENT: "Questions for Review"

5. In our competitive free-enterprise economy, everyone gains when a business is profitable. Prove this statement by showing why each of the following is interested in the company's profits:

| an investor | management | the firm's accountant |
| a consumer | union leader | tax collector |

6. How can an investor use stock market quotations to determine whether the purchase of a certain security is likely to be profitable or not?

7. How do profit rates affect the general level of economic activity?

8. What are profits used for?

9. How do government policies affect profits?

10. (a) Who really pays the corporate income tax?
    (b) Why do tax cuts usually stimulate business?
    (c) In times of recession and unemployment, which should be reduced most, corporate or individual income taxes? Explain your answer.

Evaluating Your Own Lesson

Did you achieve what you set out to do? Did your class really get the point? This is probably the most crucial phase of lesson planning. To improve your teaching of economics, you will have to be mercilessly honest with yourself in order to develop the kind of self-criticism which will enable you to improve your teaching. Self-appraisal demands that you subject yourself and your lesson to a ruthlessly critical examination *immediately after* the class session while every phase of the lesson is still fresh in mind. One way to improve one's own teaching of a specific lesson is to write comments on one's lesson plan. Which approaches, activities, and materials proved most successful? Why? Which were least successful? Why? If you will also indicate the changes you would like to make "the next time around," and if you will keep your old lesson plans on file for future reference and revision, your performance and that of your class will improve markedly. Occasionally, you might also poll your students to elicit adolescent insight into the strengths and weaknesses of specific approaches, activities, or techniques you are using.

CHECKLIST FOR SELF-EVALUATION: YOUR OWN LESSON

1. The Lesson
   A. Aim
      Was the aim of the lesson achieved?
      Was it written on the chalkboard?

Was it understood and accepted by the students?
Did the students have a share in its formulation?

B. Motivation

Was the motivation derived from student experience?
Was it appropriate?
Was it timely?
Was it challenging?
Did the teacher return to the motivation at the end of the lesson?

C. Questioning

Was the questioning effective? interesting? challenging?
Were responses one-word fragments or full-quality responses?
Were most questions "how" and "why" rather than "what" and "who"?
In a discussion lesson, did the questions arouse student-student participation rather than teacher-student participation?

D. Content

Was the methodology suitable to the content?
Did the teacher introduce new concepts, skills, and attitudes effectively?
Was the content analytical rather than descriptive?
Was the teacher teaching the "new" economics?

E. Summaries

Were *medial* and *final* summaries the result of logical steps?
Who supplied the summaries, the students or the teacher?
Did the summaries indicate mastery of the central concepts or ideas of the lesson?

F. Over-all Appraisal

Was the lesson interesting?
Did it involve the students? contribute to their development?
Was the lesson enriched? an extension of horizons?
Were the transitions from part to part smooth or artificial?
What specific changes will you make the next time around?

2. The Teacher

Were the teacher's attitude, mastery of content, and methodology inspiring?
Was the teacher in control at all times?
Were the teacher's own speech and board work in good English?
Was the teacher able to direct without monopolizing the lesson?
Were routines of housekeeping—collection and distribution of papers and materials—handled smoothly?
Were the bulletin boards effective as reflections of current study?

3. The Students

Were the students actively involved with the lesson?

Were they in rapport with the teacher?

Did they learn from the lesson?

What do you plan to do in the future to increase pupil participation in this particular economics lesson?

Conventional Methods of Teaching Economics

Until the middle of the twentieth century, economics was taught primarily by three methods: the textbook, the lecture, and the recitation. While the next few pages are devoted to the textbook, the workbook, and lectures, the emphasis in this manual is placed on inductive teaching associated with developmental-discussion techniques, the problems approach, case studies, analysis, model building, and the tools of the economist.

1.   *The Textbook Method*

During the first decades of the twentieth century, economics was taught chiefly by the textbook and the lecture methods. The textbook method followed a set formula: assignment, study, recitation, testing. The assignment was made to the textbook; study was done by the students outside of class; recitation was devoted almost entirely to questions and answers; testing was based on the information assigned.

The textbook, of course, is a valuable teaching tool. A good textbook furnishes an organized synthesis, a common core of content, and a variety of learning aids. Students should be taught how to use the textbook properly, that is, how to study from it. A teacher can accomplish this end by teaching his students how to read, how to analyze, how to outline, and how to summarize the text material. In most economics classrooms today, the teacher, with the aid of his students, superimposes on the textbook an independent organization of facts and concepts on the topic suggested by the current course of study. In modern schools, textbooks are often treated merely as a convenient teaching aid, a sort of encyclopedia.

Like the platforms of political parties, textbooks often are all things to all people. Too frequently they echo the most widely held doctrines in a manner that will offend no one. The best economics teachers consider the textbook not as the final authority, but as a convenient common source of information for the class. They understand that it is merely an outline, composed largely of generalizations and abstractions that resemble the realities of economic life as mist resembles rain. In fact, knowledgeable economics teachers today supplement the textbook with non-textbook reading materials such as biographies (Heilbroner's *Worldly Philosophers*), simple specialized accounts (Public Affairs Pamphlets), source books and books of readings, imaginative literature (Upton Sinclair's *Jungle*), reference works, and fugitive materials (chiefly booklets, pamphlets, reports and articles, usually collected by librarians in their vertical files).

However, the average economics teacher is still to a large extent dependent on his textbook. The textbook determines the scope and sequence of the course, supplies the teacher with key questions for his daily lessons, suggests problems, and provides examination questions. Even a good teacher is handicapped without a good textbook; a poorly trained teacher is lost without a very good textbook.

2. *Workbooks*

A good workbook can be a valuable supplement to the text, especially in situations in which the teacher is green, the class large, and making up absences a problem. A workbook enables a student to catch up with his fellows. An alert teacher will ask such questions as the following about his prospective workbook:

Does the workbook integrate the problems, questions, and exercises with the text?

Are the problems posed by the workbook real situations within the experience of the student?

Do the problems test analysis, problem solving, and judgment, or are they merely mechanical operations requiring the finding of the right word or phrase in the text?

Among the weaknesses of poorly constructed workbooks and, of course, work sheets designed by the teacher as well, are: lengthy reading assignments, too many hypothetical questions, unduly long questions and complicated problems, and insufficient challenge because too much work has already been done for the student.

3. *Lecture Method*

The second method, used in the early decades of the twentieth century, could be called the "funnel method." It consisted of lecturing to accompany or to supplement the time-tested formula. Its prime purpose was to explain, illustrate, or apply important principles or economic laws. This method was often highly successful with college-bound students. Pupils understood clearly what was expected of them. Concentration on information and skills made it easy for the teacher to devise valid tests and measurements. The students mastered study skills, reading skills, important definitions, and principles, and they developed an ability to organize systematically, to write lucidly, and to speak cogently in dealing with economic issues.

In recent times, with the advent of team teaching, television lessons, and advanced placement and honors classes, the lecture method has been revived. Aside from giving teachers a false sense of accomplishment, lecturing is criticized for placing the student in a passive role. He merely listens quietly, takes notes, and sometimes daydreams. Nevertheless, a well-prepared informal talk can be useful to motivate a new unit, to clarify the textbook, to review background material, and, of course, to expand the content. A dynamic lecturer can arouse interest in economics as no other media can. Moreover, a lecture may be a valuable demonstration of an intelligent man thinking analytically, rationally, and objectively about economic issues.

7 The Analytical Approach and the "New" Economics

A Rational Approach to Economic Problems

The spearhead of the multipronged attack on economic illiteracy following World War II was the National Task Force Report, *Economic Education in the Schools*. The National Task Force on Economic Education was a committee of five economists and two educators appointed in 1960 by the American Economic Association and supported by funds from the Committee for Economic Development. The primary responsibility of the Task Force was to develop a statement of "the minimum level of economics essential to good citizenship and reasonably attainable in the high schools." Some two thirds of the report, issued in October 1961, was concerned with the kind of economics that should be taught, not only in a separate economics course, but also in other courses where there is an opportunity to introduce economic materials.

The Task Force placed its first emphasis on the need for a rational approach to economic problems and devoted an entire chapter to it. The Report said, "The most important step towards understanding in economics—as in other branches of knowledge—is the replacement of emotional, unreasoned judgments by objective, rational analysis. This is the first lesson to be learned in approaching the study of economics." In short, while the student needs to acquire a modest amount of factual information about the economic world, the primary obligation of the schools is to help him develop his capacity to think clearly, objectively, and with a reasonable degree of sophistication about economic problems.

The Report stresses the character of economic choice, that is, of choosing rationally among competing alternatives. Students must be taught problem-solving techniques in the process of making choices on all levels from the personal to the national. Emphasis is placed on the steps in rational decision-making: definition of the problem, identification of ranking goals, search for alternative lines of action, and evaluation of the alternatives in terms of identified goals. In this emphasis on economics as a way of thinking, stress is placed both on the role played by personal goals (value judgments) and on the need for a set of simple analytical tools to provide guides for thinking about economic problems. Stress is laid on model building and on the importance of careful definitions and terminology.

Model Building

Some professional economists are not aware of the anxieties and uneasiness that the term "analytical approach" arouses in many social studies teachers. It conjures up nightmares of algebraic formulae, complicated charts, intricate diagrams, and other ghastly memories of the dry-as-dust, highly theoretical, abstract elementary economics course which they endured during their own college days. Since a social studies teacher probably chose to concentrate in the social sciences because he was more verbally than mathematically minded, the insecurity that this teacher suffers in a world of mathematical abstractions is compounded. However, when teachers understand that an analytical approach means simply an orderly procedure that must be followed in grappling with economic problems, much of the fear of analysis disappears. Under this approach, teachers still describe institutions and the concrete facts, but once they have secured the facts a search for the common pattern which exists among these facts should begin. The common pattern of uniformity in the facts may be called a *model*.

Engineers often build small-scale models of ships in tanks and of aircraft in wind tunnels to study the behavior of these models before constructing expensive full-scale versions. Meteorologists use other models that consist of data and equations that describe the behavior of complex weather systems with many variables. In like fashion, for the last two decades economists have constructed mathematical models to portray the complex dynamics of the American economy. The basic features of economic models are broad aggregates and sectors such as the consumer, the government, and the investment sector.[1] Actually, models are merely generalizations that have evolved from previous experience.

[1] "Economic Models: Theory on the Line," *Prospecting in Economics*, New York, the Ford Foundation, 1966, pp. 34–37.

Simple models, which constitute the economic theory the high school student needs to know, are designed to throw light on the basic structure of economics. Economic models need not be expressed in complicated mathematical symbols. The construction of a model, as Professor Evsey Domar explains it, consists of snatching from the enormous and complex mass of facts called reality a few simple, easily manageable key points which, when put together in some "cunning" way, become for certain purposes a substitute for reality itself. Simplification is the heart of the process.[2]

The Rationale of a K–12 Approach to Economic Understandings

In New York City and other places using the K–12 approach, the rationale of the latest revision of economic understandings and skills from kindergarten through the twelfth grade is based on the learning theories of Dr. Jerome S. Bruner, Director of the Center of Cognitive Studies and Professor of Psychology, Harvard University.

In *The Process of Education* and other writings, Dr. Bruner has developed the following ideas:[3]

First, each natural and social science has basic organizing principles, facts, and assumptions which, in his view, form its structure. If the basic structure of the discipline is presented *first* to the student by the teacher and understood by the student, all subsequent learning of content is facilitated because by mastering structure the student learns how things are related. In short, an understanding of the basic generalizations and broad ideas of the discipline helps students to organize the facts, principles, and assumptions of economics into meaningful, connected patterns.

Second, the principles, general truths, or concepts of a discipline like economics can be made understandable to all levels of comprehension provided that they are presented in a context which the child understands. Moreover, it is assumed that most children are capable of applying simple analytical reasoning to problems within their ken.

Third, to achieve this kind of mastery, a spiral curriculum should be introduced for economic understandings and skills. Earlier education,

---

[2] Evsey Domar, *Essays in the Theory of Economic Growth.* New York, Oxford University Press, 1957, p. 22 f.

[3] Jerome S. Bruner, *The Process of Education.* Cambridge, Massachusetts, Harvard University Press, 1960; and *On Knowing: Essays for the Left Hand.* Cambridge, Massachusetts, Harvard University Press, 1962.

of necessity, is on a simpler level, but its focus is still on basic structure. Later, education moves on to a more difficult and a more complicated level where there is a "continual broadening and deepening of knowledge in terms of basic and general ideas."

Fourth, learning should be based on inquiry and discovery. The child should be encouraged to figure out for himself regularities in his physical and socio-political environments. Children enjoy formulating plausible hypotheses about human interactions.

Fifth, students must be taught to generalize. Relating concepts to the fundamental structure or pattern of the discipline aids retention. Bruner said, "perhaps the most basic thing that can be said about human memory . . . is that unless it is placed into a structure or pattern it is rapidly forgotten. . . ."

Economic Analysis

A basic premise, therefore, of the rationale of economic education is that students will acquire knowledge of the structure and mechanics of the economic world through training in simple economic analysis and through the development of basic concepts, buttressed by the latest economic facts.

The process of economic analysis has two major aspects. The first is an objective, rational explanation of the facts with respect to an economic event or condition and the implications of the event or condition. The second is the utilization of this explanation in decision-making. For example, by the process of economic analysis a student is able to explain correctly why a certain event or condition occurred in the past, why it exists now, and what may possibly be done, or what might have been done, to change it. Specifically, he can explain why the market price of wheat, for example, is what it is at a given time by considering the quantities and prices in the demand schedule at the time. The raw factual data of economics probably change more rapidly than those of any other area of social studies teaching. To attempt to master or to keep up with new data in economics is fruitless. Since one cannot predict the economic problems students will be called upon to react to in the future, the professional economist insists that it is imperative for the student to master the analytical tools of the discipline so that he will know how to apply general principles to any specific situation which may arise.

The Analytical Tools

Three sets of analytical tools are required to impart the skills which are essential to effective economic analysis.

The first set relates to history, the study which provides us with present-day and past facts, empirical data, and perspective. An understanding of the historic process helps the economics student to understand the origin, functions, growth, or decline of important economic institutions. Further, history helps students comprehend how institutions adjust to changes in technology and to the growth or depletion of various resources.

The second set of analytical tools consists of skill in the use of statistical procedures and concepts, a skill which enables us to quantify and to compare important economic facts. Knowing how to use and not to abuse statistics is an essential skill for economic analysis.

The third set of indispensable techniques for analysis is concerned with theory. Theory involves model building as a means of identifying the key elements within a complex whole and putting the facts and ideas together in the meaningful, logical, cause-and-effect relation which structures economics and makes it a scientific discipline.

In *Changing Emphases in Social Studies Affecting Curriculum Change*, M. L. Frankel, Director of the Joint Council on Economic Education, suggests several topics that can be taught effectively through analysis with the help of the tools of the economist:

1. The nature and growth of corporations,
2. The economies of scale in giant corporations,
3. The professionalization of management and its relationship to ownership and control in corporations,
4. The role of economics in the power structure of American society,
5. The effects of mass production on American economic, cultural, and political patterns, and
6. The changing nature of competition.

Such topics, and others which Dr. Frankel mentions, highlight constant change as the major characteristic and strength of American society. Frankel concedes that teaching understanding is time-consuming but using time "to think about some of the content in depth pays great dividends to the student." [4]

[4] M. L. Frankel, *Changing Emphases in Social Studies Affecting Curriculum Change*. New York, Joint Council on Economic Education, 1962, pp. 12–15.

Conceptual Learning

Although teachers speak glibly of teaching economic concepts, both the precise meaning of the term "concept" and the procedure for teaching a concept are often nebulous. In pedagogical literature, the meaning of "concept" ranges from an idea of a specific and limited nature to a broad generalization. In this chapter, it is defined simply as an abstract idea that is understood within the experience of the student. Economic concepts can be introduced in simplified versions in the elementary grades and taught in progressively more complex variations in succeeding grades because, as the child's level of learning deepens, the understandings associated with the concept also expand. For example, "In an exchange economy, money is necessary; barter will not work" is a fourth-grade level of understanding of the concept of money. But as the child's knowledge of American history increases, the concept of money can be expanded to encompass the idea that there is a relationship between the money supply and prices. The child can now understand that, as the money supply increases, prices usually rise; as the money supply decreases, prices usually fall.

In the early 1960's, state departments of education and individual public school systems devised conceptual frameworks for the social studies which list major concepts in economics, history, and the other social studies, and the grade level (K–12) at which these concepts should be introduced. Since, in the late 1960's, economics is probably able to conceptualize its basic theoretical framework (structure) more effectively than any other social study, economics can make an important contribution to educational methodology by demonstrating to teachers of social studies the procedures and advantages of conceptual teaching. In economics, as in other subject areas, it is important to ask not, "What's this?" but to inquire "What's going on here and why?" For the first question strings together facts in a descriptive pattern; the second question emphasizes the process and the importance of concepts. Understanding increasingly must emerge from today's mass of facts. Concepts or ideas must provide a framework along which facts can find meaningful paths.

How to Teach a Concept

How does one teach the concept that insurance companies are a stabilizing force in the American economy? *A Teacher's Guide to Economics in the Business Education Curriculum* suggests that a concept can be considered "the result of reflective thinking on two or more understandings." To teach how the insurance industry helps to stabilize our economy, the teacher must first teach the following basic understandings.

1. Insurance is based upon a mutual sharing of risks.
2. Insurance helps to maintain the family as a social institution in times of adversity.
3. Planned insurance programs enable individuals to build substantial estates.
4. Insurance companies try to promote thrift in many ways.

After reflecting on these four understandings, students should be encouraged to generalize about what they have learned in this portion of the lesson. Indeed, by way of medial summary, the teacher might ask: "In seeking profits for themselves, how do private insurance companies help the economy as a whole as well as themselves?" In the discussion which will follow, one or more students will soon zero in on the economic significance of the insurance business as a stabilizing force in the American economy.

Why should economics teachers stress basic concepts, such as this one, rather than a multitude of facts about Prudential, John Hancock, or Metropolitan Life? Facts change with the passage of time. Furthermore, isolated factual material is soon forgotten. But concepts, because they are in the nature of reasoned conclusions, are less susceptible to change and therefore are of a more enduring nature.

A word of caution: In one's enthusiasm for conceptual learning, one must never forget that sound concepts are built on a solid foundation of facts. Facts are needed both for an adequate understanding of persistent economic problems and for intelligent decision-making on economic issues. The facts which the high school economics teacher stresses are of little lasting value unless they are used in further study and analysis. Until students have gained experience in the study of economics, they will need help in sorting, sifting, and assessing factual information. Only thus will they learn to separate the significant grain of truth from the chaff of popular writing on economics.

Effective teachers of economics teach concepts by using several "languages" concurrently: clear oral prose, brief written prose on the chalkboard, geometric drawing, and sometimes graphic and algebraic presentation. To be taught effectively, concepts must be relevant and ongoing and used explicitly in a variety of situations at different points in the course or curriculum. A student has not really understood a concept until he can express it in most of the several languages of economics and until he is able to apply the concept to new situations.[5]

[5] Laurence E. Leamer, *The Economist as Teacher: Informal Essays on the Collegiate Teaching of Economics*, Monograph C–13. Cincinnati, South-Western Publishing Company, 1965, p. 58.

Concepts in the One-Semester Twelfth-Grade Economics Course

At the high school level, under the K–12 approach, the teacher should stress concepts relating to capitalism, free enterprise, competition, administered prices, fiscal policy, comparative economic systems, and so on. He must deepen and enrich the concepts, introduced previously, that increased productivity makes possible the greater satisfaction of man's wants, that increased trade results from interdependence, and that capital is the key factor in producing goods which consumers want. The high school student must understand that societies develop economic systems to allocate limited resources, that decision-making on the use of limited resources is the basis of every economic system, whether it be capitalism, socialism, or communism, and that changes in a private-enterprise economy like ours result from decisions made by consumers, producers, and government. Lawrence Senesh has said that a projection of the economic world through the teaching of basic concepts can serve as a frame of reference that will be useful from the earliest schooldays throughout adult life. This conceptual framework serves as a strong foundation upon which teachers in succeeding grades can build. Early economic experience, rooted in the child's familiar environment, can thus spiral as his environment expands to encompass the national scene and even the world.

To sum up, Dr. Bruner's ideas of pattern, structure, basic concepts, and discovery and inquiry techniques provide the basis of the analytical approach to the teaching of economic understanding. His ideas are also at the root of the controversy as to the kind of economics which can and should be taught to students on both the elementary and secondary school levels.

CHAPTER

8   *Economic Analysis Through Developmental-Discussion Techniques*

The Developmental-Discussion Lesson

A developmental-discussion-type lesson is a lesson in which the students attempt cooperatively to find solutions to a problem which the class has accepted as worthy of study. As its name implies, its main and subordinate concepts are developed through a half-dozen stimulating, thought-provoking pivotal questions which serve as the basis for class discussion. Properly constructed, these key or pivotal questions, when they are analyzed by the students under the guidance of the teacher, will bring under discussion the essential concepts connected with the problem for the day.

The following example illustrates how a pivotal or key question differs from a straight factual question.

TOPIC: How does a monopolist fix prices?

Factual Question	*Pivotal or Key Question*
1. What is meant by monopoly?	1. You own a local movie house with 400 seats. Each performance costs $100. How will you decide whether to charge 50¢, 75¢, or $1 for admission?

Factual Question	*Pivotal or Key Question*
	a. How might your price policy have to change if the parish church has well-attended bingo parties?
	b. Why might a smart owner avoid charging a dollar even if he filled the house almost every night?
2. How does a monopolist fix prices?	2. Homework problem involving the demand schedule for a patented window-cleaning device.
	a. Why do sales drop from 500 to 200 when the price rises from 50¢ to $1?
	b. If the product were safety glass required on all cars by law, would the same decline occur?
	c. In which case would the government be more likely to intervene? Why?
3. Why can't a monopolist fix his selling price at the highest possible level?	3. How do these methods of determining price differ from the method used by a truck farmer?
4. What is the difference between monopoly price and competitive price?	4. Why do the methods differ?

The developmental-discussion method keeps the discussion relevant to a few fixed targets, forcing the students to distinguish facts from opinion and to use their newly acquired analytical tools whenever appropriate. John R. Coleman said that this kind of teaching is difficult. It is inspiring when it is done by experts who know their subject and their students but sham when done by others.[1]

---

[1] John R. Coleman, "Second Thoughts on Economics in the Schools," *Social Education*, 29:74–78 (February 1965).

Motivation—Springboard to the Lesson

The purposes of motivation is to arouse and sustain the kind of interest that promotes self-activity. Earlier, the author pointed out that the developmental tasks of youth are intrinsically motivating. A sagacious teacher integrates his economics lessons with his students' personal concerns: to graduate and thus achieve adult status; to earn grades high enough to assure admission to college; to understand the world in which he lives; to be more popular, knowledgeable, and attractive; and to have a part in making a better world and a better tomorrow. In a developmental lesson, effective motivation serves three purposes.

1. By arousing, enhancing, and sustaining interest, it creates a desire to solve the problem involved in the lesson.
2. By eliciting and clarifying the aim, it makes the lesson purposeful.
3. By evoking a number of student responses, it sets the tone for the lesson and builds a solid foundation for further discussion.

The following are a few of the ways of motivating an economics lesson:

Motivational Device	*Example*
Personalizing the problem	How would you prepare for an interview for a summer job?
Utilizing students' personal experiences	Should a high school teen-age band join the Musicians' Union? Why?
Challenging question	Should recipients of poverty program benefits form a union to increase those benefits?
Quotations	Extracts from books, speeches, and Presidential messages.
Cartoons	Sources: Scholastic Magazines transparencies, Public Affairs Pamphlets, *The New York Times* student supplements.
Source materials	Example: The Omaha Platform of the Populist Party.
Charts, tables, graphs	Sources: *U.S. News & World Report,* Scholastic Magazines transparencies.
Anecdotes	Account of the Triangle Shirtwaist Company fire.

Motivational Device	*Example*
Pictures	Sources: *Life, Look,* pictorial histories.
Newspaper headlines	Congress Enacts Medicare for Aged.
Student opinion polls	Should medicare be extended downward to fifty-year-olds?
It might have happened	If World War II had been followed by a worldwide depression such as that of 1929, what might have happened in the United States?

Achievement in a Single Period

A developmental-discussion-type lesson attempts to achieve its aim in a single class period. Formulating the aim for a developmental lesson, however, is no easy task. A good aim has the following characteristics: it is appropriate to the needs and abilities of the class; it is, if possible, phrased as a problem; it tends to create and excite interest; and it serves as the focal point for the organization of the content. Aims are more stimulating if they emphasize the controversial aspects of a problem. It is better to phrase the aim of a lesson on government regulation of public utilities in terms of *whether* regulation was inevitable rather than *why* it was inevitable. Knowledgeable teachers understand that, when students are involved in formulating the aim of the lesson for the day, they are more likely to understand and accept the challenge of solving it.

Provocative Pivotal Questions

The backbone of the developmental lesson is, as we have just observed, a series of concrete, thought-provoking, sequential pivotal questions. The answers that the students and the teacher working cooperatively in a "creative encounter" provide for these key questions should be the outline of the factual content of the lesson. Pivotal questions should be personalized to insure "you-appeal" and involvement, vary as to source and to kind, and, above all, be interesting. Of course, like all questions, key questions should be simple, direct, and logical and should make good use of student response.

The checklist that follows points out the criteria of good questions and good questioning techniques.

CHECKLIST: THE ART OF QUESTIONING

I. Mechanics
 1. Do you allow for a pause so that the question will "sink in" before calling on a student to answer it?
 2. Do you direct your question to the entire class before singling out a person to answer it?
 3. Do you distribute questions widely among volunteers and draftees?
 4. Do you formulate your pivotal questions in advance in your lesson plan?

II. Effective Questioning Techniques
 1. Do you ask questions that require analysis and critical thinking?
 2. Do some of your questions call for comparisons or contrasts?
 3. Do you ask personalized questions that involve students in the situation under discussion?
 4. Are your questions thought-provoking or do they require memorization of the textbook?
 5. Do some of your questions elicit cause-and-effect relationships?
 6. Do you formulate your aim as a problem expressed as a question?
 7. Do you encourage several students to contribute to the answer to a single pivotal question?
 8. Do you turn back to the class student questions that are germane to the discussion?

III. Treatment of Answers
 1. Do your students understand that their answers are meant for the entire class and not exclusively for you?
 2. Do you require students to speak audibly, correctly, and to the class?
 3. Do you repeat students' answers? [1]
 4. Do you engage in controversies with individual students while the rest of the class remains silent?

---

[1] This is a bad practice, since if you do it repeatedly, students will not listen the first time you ask the question.

IV. Pitfalls in Questioning

Pitfall	*Example*
1. Double or multiple questions	1. How did Theodore Roosevelt handle industrial combinations and why was he called a "trust buster"? Why did he smash the Standard Oil Trust?
2. Questions inviting one-word answers	2. Did the Sherman Antitrust Act of 1890 illustrate the laissez-faire attitude of the federal government?
3. The whiplash question	3. Franklin D. Roosevelt tried to "pack the Supreme Court" and lost *when?*
4. The leading question	4. Don't you think that the Vietnam War curtailed Lyndon Johnson's Great Society program?
5. The vague or ambiguous question	5. What happened in 1933? How are the Great Society and the Fair Deal alike?
6. The guessing question	6. Was the Sherman Antitrust Act the first example of social control by the federal government?
7. Verbose questions	7. Why is the consumer called a king and a very potent force in the market when he exercises his regal powers and shouldn't he?
8. The indefinite or elliptical question	8. How about President Johnson's War on Poverty?
9. The chorus-answer question	9. Class, who signed the Employment Act of 1946?
10. The teacher-addressed question	10. Can anyone tell *me* why open market operations are used by the Open Market Committee of the Federal Reserve System?

Development Through Selected Meaningful Content

A common mistake of economics teachers in preparing a lesson plan for a developmental-discussion lesson is thinking in terms of an outline of facts rather than considering for emphasis the significant ideas and large problems inherent in the lesson. High school teachers of economics should not attempt to teach the economist's economics. Rather, they must select those concepts, institutions, and models from the discipline of economics that will be meaningful to high school boys and girls. The process of relating the content of the lesson to a theme that is taught in a logical, sequential way has been aptly called "creative-power teaching." After the content has illustrated the theme, the theme must be applied to matters which are important to the student today, if the lesson is to have lasting effect. In short, the proponents of developmental-discussion techniques firmly believe that they produce a more durable educational experience than a "re-citation" based on memoriter methods and textbook materials.

CHECKLIST: CRITERIA FOR GOOD LESSON DEVELOPMENT
1. Do you have a carefully prepared lesson plan?
2. Is your development logical and sequential?
3. Do you attempt to connect the present lesson with previously learned material through review or some other device?
4. Do you attempt to bring the previous night's homework assignment into the lesson?
5. Are your transitions smooth?
6. Have you planned a variety of activities to encourage pupil participation?
7. Is yours a truly socialized approach?
8. Do you have a suggested time allotment for each part of your lesson?
9. Do you provide for occasional change of pace?
10. Have you exercised both the courage to exclude and the imagination to include certain content in your lesson?

Use of Illustrative Devices

Every lesson can be greatly improved by the use of visual and auditory materials because such materials make learning experiences richer, deeper, more realistic, and more memorable. Since visual and auditory techniques offer great opportunities for improving learning, the developmental lesson uses them for achieving the major purposes of good teaching, whenever possible. The chalkboard or flannel board for diagrams and notes, transparencies and overlays for enhanced visual appeal, and realia such as stocks, bonds, and ticker tape—all add pertinence, accuracy, and interest to a lesson. A teacher can integrate with his lesson for the day films, filmstrips, television programs, or tapes previously seen or heard by his students.

Medial and Final Summaries

In a successful developmental lesson, the content (concepts, principles, understandings, and skills) must be presented vividly and effectively in the first place. Usually this is accomplished best by developing a running summary outline on the chalkboard with the active participation of the students in arriving at the items. A good summary outline not only has visual appeal but it also organizes the material so that students can see the major ideas in their proper relationship. The board notes should be copied in the students' notebooks for the following reasons.

1. Copying the outline contributes to mastery of the essential facts.
2. A good set of notes is valuable for review.
3. Students learn how to make a logical and effective outline.

A good summary has the following characteristics.

1. It clinches the chief concepts in the lesson.
2. It refers back, as a rule, to both the aim and the motivation.
3. It is stated by a student rather than by the teacher.
4. It is interesting and novel.

Application

The content of a creative developmental-discussion-type lesson should be related to the theme of the lesson. Even though a teacher has taught the causes of and the cures for the Great Depression of 1929 in a logical, sequential, and effective manner, he has not really made his lesson an effective learning experience until the class has "generalized" the thesis. The class must also apply the analytical concepts or the model that it has developed to the causes of, and cures for, depressions in general. Although you are interested in teaching large ideas, principles, or themes, your lesson cannot be thin in facts. There can be no effective educational growth or maturity in viewpoint without sound scholarship.

Development Through Student Preparation

The success of today's developmental lesson is determined by the way in which the assignment was made yesterday and carried out by the students at home. A well-prepared assignment assures good class discussion.

CHECKLIST: CRITERIA FOR A GOOD ASSIGNMENT

1. Is the assignment clear, definite, understood by each student?
2. Does it have a worthy purpose acceptable to both the teacher and the students?
3. Does it link the past with the present and point to the future?
4. Is it concerned with one of the "developmental tasks of youth"?
5. Is it reasonable and possible of attainment?
6. Do you check up on how it was done?
7. Does it make provision for individual differences in the ability levels of students?
8. Does the assignment emphasize essentials? stimulate confidence that it can be accomplished? anticipate difficulties?
9. In making the assignment do you tell the student not only what to learn but also how to go about learning it?
10. Does it provide a checking device or standard of measurement so the student will know whether or not he has successfully carried out the assignment?
11. Do you show a lively interest in the assignment?
12. Do you allow sufficient time to motivate your assignments?

Economics assignments usually consist of set problems to solve rather than a given number of pages to read. Understandings and concepts learned in problem solving are more likely to be retained. Assignments may be short- or long-range. Preparation for the unit on "The Growth of Big Business" may engage the students' attention for a week or more. A lesson on "Forms of Business Organization: the Single Proprietor, Partnership, and Corporation" may occupy students for just a day or two. Assignments like this one are called short-range. Preparation for participation in a forum, or writing a position paper, a book review, or a term paper, on the other hand, are long-range assignments.

Assignments may have a variety of purposes.

1. *To find material:* Students may be asked to interview a union member regarding a current local labor dispute, to read the stock mar-

ket page to determine how the stocks of a local corporation are faring, to bring in samples of emotional advertising or clippings from the newspaper on urban economic problems.

2. *To organize knowledge:* Such an assignment involves outlining a topic or preparing a brief in support of, or opposed to, such measures as anti-cigarette legislation, a state lottery, or an income-tax cut.

3. *To evaluate evidence:* An assignment of this kind is concerned with problem-solving. It can be accomplished through the writing of a two-page position paper on topics such as Foreign Aid to the Middle East: How Much?; The Elimination of Discrimination in Employment; Should Mass Media Cigarette Advertising Be Banned?

4. *To illustrate the topic:* Cartoons, flow charts, or tables can illustrate the topic that the class is currently discussing.

For example, students may be asked to draw a cartoon to illustrate the effects of inflation on the Sunday dinner of a middle-income family. They may construct a simple flow chart depicting money flow from factories to families by way of wages and salaries and the return of this money when families pay for goods and services. Or they may compile a table showing the principal imports and exports of the world's ten leading trading nations.

Lesson Plan for a Developmental Lesson

TOPIC: How Do Americans Try to Solve the Problem of Economic Insecurity?

AIMS: 1. To show how our modern economic system has fostered insecurity
   2. To point out that both the individual and the government have a responsibility to provide a degree of economic security
   3. To reenforce skills of analysis and critical thinking

MOTIVATION:

In savage tribes where skulls are thick and primal passions rage,
They have a system sure and quick to cure the blight of age.
For when a native's youth has fled and age has sapped his vim,
They simply knock him on the head and put an end to him.

But we in our enlightened age are built of nobler stuff,
And so we look with scorn and rage on deeds so harsh and rough.
And when a man is old and gray, and stooped and short of breath,
We simply take his job away and let him starve to death!

QUESTIONS ON THE MOTIVATION:

How can you tell that this verse was written before the Franklin D. Roosevelt Administration?

Has social security in the form of old-age pensions, unemployment insurance, and medicare solved the problem of insecurity? Explain your answer.

What, then, should be the main concern in our economics lesson today?

[Many teachers draw up in advance mimeographed assignments for an entire unit or even for the course. Spirit-duplicated or mimeographed assignment sheets save time, insure accuracy, enable students to make up work if they have been absent, and may provide the teacher with opportunities to include quotations, statistics, charts, and even an occasional cartoon for interpretation.]

Content Outline	*Pivotal Questions*
I. The Industrial Revolution created toolless, often craftless, workers dependent on their employers for their livelihood.	One hundred years ago, the average American rarely worried about "insecurity" in his old age. In 1968, security is an obsession. Why?

II. "Four fears" haunt the average workman today
  a. Ill-health and disability
  b. Advancing age
  c. Death—fear of leaving his family in want
  d. Unemployment
	When a factory worker kisses his wife goodbye in the morning, he leaves haunted by fears. What are they? Why does each one trouble him?

III. Kinds of unemployment
  a. Cyclical—business fluctuations
  b. Seasonal—Good Humor Man
  c. Secular—changes in consumer habits
  d. Technological—automation
	In an agricultural society unemployment does not exist: There is always too much to do. In an industrial society, however, the worker is faced with a variety of types of unemployment. What are they? Why are there differences between the two societies?

IV. Ways of providing for one's own security	How can a factory worker provide a degree of security for his family on his own?

Content Outline	Pivotal Questions
a. Savings. Can everyone save?	
b. Buying insurance, annuities	
c. Keeping health through good food and right living	
d. Joining cooperatives and medical plans	*Medial Summary:* How can Mr. and Mrs. Newly Wed anticipate insecurity problems in their married life?
V. Ways in which a company provides security for workers	How can a company protect an employee against some of the hazards of modern life?
a. Company group insurance	
b. G.A.W. and S.U.B. Plans	
c. Fringe benefits—hospitalization	
VI. Social insurance	How do the federal and state governments take responsibility for some of the hazards in an industrial society?
a. Social Security Act of 1935 and Amendments—Old-age, survivors', disability, and unemployment insurance	Why has government stepped in to deal with this problem?
b. Medicare for aged	

SUMMARY: You are planning a talk to be given to the Discussion Club of your school on "Insecurity in 1968." What items would you discuss in your talk? Why?

APPLICATION: Mexico has invited you to plan a social security system for its growing industrial population. What role would you expect the state to play? What burdens should the individual worker in Mexico assume? Why?

9 Economic Analysis Through the Problems Approach

Controversial Issues in Economics

William H. Kilpatrick once said, "If one's teaching is really to promote the role of intelligence, it cannot proceed by indoctrination, but only by open-minded study." Problem-oriented instruction deals with controversy, that is, with those issues about which honest men have differences of opinion. One of the major purposes of teaching economics is to help the student grow into an effective, well-informed citizen who understands questions of public policy and contributes to their solution through the formation of public opinion. "Problems," says Laurence Leamer, Professor of Economics at Harpur College, "provide the basis for economics."

Problems arise out of conflicting goals. An economic problem exists whenever people, seeking to obtain abundance, economic growth, stability, security, or economic justice, propose solutions which conflict with the cherished beliefs, economic interests, or group affiliations of a part of the citizenry. Specific issues about which there are actual or potential conflicts of opinion include the war on poverty, blighted urban areas, discrimination in jobs and housing, and the raising of state revenues by lotteries. Some teachers in the past have considered such topics to be closed areas of culture, that is, not a subject for analytical classroom study. Others have tried to steer clear of the problems approach because problem-solving involves controversy, and controversy arouses emotions. Still others have straddled the issue by presenting balanced lists of arguments for and arguments against controversial proposals, such as the negative income tax or participation by recipients of relief in community poverty projects. But these unresolved problems of public policy are the very issues with which free men must grapple in order to make wise choices that constitute "the excitement that is economics." A candid approach to controversial issues cannot be avoided, however, if the economics teacher is to fulfill his educational purpose.

Controversial Issues in the Classroom

After an economist has defined an economic problem, he often proposes several possible solutions to it. The choice which a citizen makes among the alternative solutions gives rise to much of the controversy that makes economics so fascinating, so perplexing, and so infuriating to many people. John Kenneth Galbraith has said that controversial public issues provide us with both "the bread and butter of political controversy" and "our daily diet of insinuation, indignation and insult." It is, of course, next to impossible—perhaps undesirable as well—to suppress the expression of attitudes, ideals, and even personal prejudices that sway students' decisions. As an economics teacher learns the personal predilections of the individual boys and girls in his class, and as he trains his students in parliamentary procedure, critical thinking, and suspended judgment, he will be increasingly able to cope successfully with the heat and fury of a class aroused. The alternative to controversy in the classroom is the absence of feeling, which the professional economist may hail as the rational, the analytical approach, but which a high school teacher usually finds indicative of apathy, boredom, and indifference.

Steps in Problem-Solving

The National Task Force on Economic Education recommended that economics on the high school level should stress "a rational way of thinking about economic problems." According to the Task Force, the "rational way" involves four steps: "First, we must define the problem. . . . Second, we must identify our goals. . . . Third, we must look for the principal alternative ways of attaining these objectives. . . . Fourth, we must analyze the consequences of choosing each possible line of action. . . ."

Students should be taught early in the semester that all boys and girls are not expected to reach the same conclusion because there is no one and only solution to the major economic problems of our day. If all members of an economics class customarily reach identical solutions on controversial issues, an economics teacher should reexamine his objectives, motives, and educational procedures. *A Teacher's Guide to Economics in the Business Education Curriculum* (published jointly by the Joint Council on Economic Education and the National Business Education Association) summarizes this point: "Differences of opinion are not only natural but are also indicative of varied and vigorous thinking."

Teaching Personal Security Through the Problems Approach

Although the four steps suggested by the National Task Force are fundamental, the details and the refinements of each step in the problem-solving approach to teaching high school economics will vary from teacher to teacher. The problem chosen for study should arouse interest; involve a critical issue, that is, one which students can associate with their own experience and thoughts; and, above all, be one to which the methods of economic analysis can be applied. The developmental-discussion-type lesson is ideally suited to the problems approach.

Obviously, the first step is to recognize and to define the problem. One can recognize an economic problem by discovering its symptoms—demonstrations, strikes, investigations, and protests from pressure groups. In teaching Personal Security in the United States via the problems approach, the teacher should first present various aspects of insecurity in America in order that the students may be able to answer the basic question, "Who are the American poor?" Naturally, at this stage of the discussion, the teacher and his class must come to an agreement regarding the scope of the problem which they are to study.

The students are now ready for the second step; that is, they are now in a position to define the problem: "How does a twentieth-century American cope with problems of insecurity?"

The third step consists of discussing and weighing alternatives. At this stage, the class should examine data describing Lyndon B. Johnson's war on poverty, the goals of the Great Society, changing attitudes toward personal security, and a host of personal, union, company, and governmental efforts to provide a modicum of personal security in a complex industrialized society. Of course, while individual efforts are highlighted, the role of social security must be emphasized.

The fourth step involves a tentative solution. The class will probably conclude that social security is an indispensable requisite of the American free-enterprise economy.

Persistent Economic Problems

In 1953, Edwin G. Nourse, chairman of the first Council of Economic Advisors, appointed by President Harry S. Truman under the Employment Act of 1946, wrote an article for *Social Education* entitled "Persistent Problems of the American Economy," which he prepared specifically for high school teachers. The five broad persistent problems Dr. Nourse described in his rather lengthy article were:

I. Our Natural Resources, Their Conservation, Use and Development
II. Our Labor Force, Its Development and Utilization
III. The Need for Capital and the Means of Supplying It
IV. Forms of Business Organization and Management
V. Government and Economic Life[1]

Each of these problems has a half dozen or more sub-headings. "Altogether, the article," Wesley and Wronski tell us, "contributes an invaluable review and digest of economic understanding."

In 1966, Dr. Nourse wrote another article for *Social Education* entitled "Current Aspects of Our Persistent Economic Problems," in which he updated his list. To his 1953 list, he added the world-wide population dilemma, the potential of "laboristic-capitalism," and the changing relationship between government and business in the late 1960's.[2] Dr. Nourse cautioned us that "problems which will persist in an ever-changing society" often need new perspectives and foresight for their solution.

A careful reading of both of Dr. Nourse's articles will provide the teacher of economics with a fruitful list of major economic problems, including a number of interrelated minor problems under the half dozen or so sub-headings. Both articles, of course, furnish descriptive detail, insights, analysis, and policy proposals for the solution of each of the persistent problems.

[1] *Social Education,* 17:297–311 (November 1953).
[2] *Social Education,* 30:232–235 (April 1966).

Appraisal of the Problems Approach

The problems approach serves several purposes.

1. It applies general principles to concrete situations and enriches the process of education.

2. It captures the imagination, and the hope of finding a solution is a powerful inducement to study and investigation.

3. It makes the high school course more analytical and less descriptive because it follows an inductive approach to learning.

4. It introduces students to some of the economists' tools and techniques.

5. It provides experience in analysis and enables the teacher to develop interest in important issues.

One word of caution: A series of lessons using the problems approach must be well organized since much time will be consumed on motivational devices, the provision of descriptive and institutional background, and individual research.

10 *Economic Analysis Through Case Studies: A Variant of the Problems Approach*

What Is a Case Study?

In the language of educational magic, the term *case study* frequently denotes innovation. Actually, the case-study method is nothing new. For years it has been standard procedure at the graduate level to use actual cases for instructional purposes in economics, law, business, medicine, political science, and international affairs. Case studies are generally investigations which are limited to a single problem, action, decision, or institution rather than an analysis of a large number of phenomena. Proponents of the case-study approach usually assume, however, that examination of a limited incident, condition, or event will yield conclusions that may be validly applied to a more general class of similar incidents, conditions, or events.

On the high school level, a case study is usually based on readings in source books or in current periodicals such as *U.S. News & World Report, Business Week, Time,* or *Newsweek;* or it takes the form of a spirit-duplicated or mimeographed handout, prepared by the teacher. Teachers agree that a case study should go beyond typical workbook techniques. A case study, of course, involves a careful, concise textual description of an economic condition, institution, or industry.

Planning a Case Study

After the student or teacher has identified the importance of the problem involved in the case study, the main concepts and their import should be arrived at analytically. Indeed, the purpose of introducing simple case studies on the high school level is progressively to widen the range and to increase the depth of the students' understanding of economic analysis. The emphasis in case studies should be on active student involvement via learning by doing. Ideally, the readings in current periodicals, the source book, and the handouts should be interwoven with the text and the cases organized around the basic tools and concepts of economic analysis. A teacher who prepares his own case studies and presents them to his students as handouts should draw upon a variety of illustrative devices—cartoons, statistical data, descriptions of real-life problems, all of which call for an economic solution.

Case studies should be short, limited to two or three major issues, and drawn from a variety of sources. Questions at the end of each selection help to focus the students' attention on the point at issue. A good case study based on a real situation sometimes raises questions which are incentives to further investigation. It may even result in a term paper, consisting of a series of case studies in which the student arrives at generalizations or basic conclusions which are based on evidence and analysis.

Economics teachers can use case studies for topics such as TVA and Appalachia, the Farm Problem in the Union of Soviet Socialist Republics and the United States, Medicare, Junior Achievement, or the economics of the General Organization Store.

A career book on nursing, social work, or teaching resembles a case study. Girls often will select this as an alternative to a term paper and do very well with it.

Organizing a mock corporation in class is also an excellent device for teaching various aspects of the business world. The Tom Thumb Toy Corporation issues stocks and bonds, elects officers, and conducts business. The mock corporation can be used throughout the term to illustrate the effects of overhead costs, labor, tax policies, and other problems.

Styles and Uses of Case Studies

In their article "Case Study Approaches in Social Studies," [1] Fred M. Newmann and Donald W. Oliver describe different styles and uses of case studies, with interesting and colorful illustrations selected from the unit on Labor which they are developing experimentally as a part of the Harvard Social Studies Project. The style of the case studies used in their article includes:

1. *Stories* (to portray authentic or fictitious events)
2. *Vignettes* (to present a "short excerpt or slice of experience")
3. *Journalistic Historical Narrative* (to describe the actions of individuals or institutions)
4. *Documents* (to introduce original sources)
5. *Research Data* (to test factual claims)
6. *Short Texts* (to explain reasons, trends)
7. *Interpretative Essays* (to evaluate evidence and reach conclusions on abstract issues).

In their article, Professors Newmann and Oliver also state that case-study materials serve at least two general purposes: (1) "to illustrate foregone conclusions," and (2) "to provide controversy and debate on issues for which 'true' conclusions do not yet exist." Both categories involve "what people should have done or ought to do."

The Role of the Teacher

In "Using Case Studies in Social Studies Classes," William F. Dinwiddie cautions that the role of the teacher "needs to be carefully defined." [2] After assigning a case study for analysis, the teacher serves as a resource person and discussion leader. He may, of course, occasionally present ideas of his own to the class but he should avoid dominating the discussion. Dinwiddie suggests the following classroom procedure.

1. A *clarification phase* of the discussion during which the facts of the case are presented and understood by all
2. A discussion of the *issues* in the case during which the controversial points involved openly or covertly are aired
3. A *decision-making* phase during which the class decides what, if anything, can be done and what policy is best and why

[1] *Social Education*, 31:108–113 (February 1967).
[2] William F. Dinwiddie, "Using Case Studies in Social Studies Classes," *Social Education*, 31:397–400 (May 1967).

In the decision-making stage, there is no need to try to force a consensus or for all to agree on one best policy. Decision-making enables the students to engage in economic analysis. The students must begin by examining their own values and assumptions, for values and assumptions often influence decisions. Then the alternatives should be thoughtfully considered and the consequences of each course of action carefully weighed before the decision is made final.

As discussion leader, the teacher should avoid acting as if he were a referee in a fight or a propagandist for a certain point of view. Rather, he should try to get all points of view fairly represented so that the students working cooperatively can come to conclusions acceptable to themselves individually. The teacher can help in this process by encouraging students to make choices freely, using a reasoned, unemotional analytical approach. The main objective of the case-study method of instruction is to help the students learn how to think for themselves.

How to Teach a Case Study

Kenneth Boulding once said: "The task of economic analysis is to set forth before man as clearly as possible the alternatives among which he must choose." The following case study attempts to apply Boulding's definition. It confronts the student with hypothetical proposals for the solution of a real problem faced by the residents of a suburban community. Each student is expected to receive his own mimeographed copy of the case study, and each is expected to write out his responses, or, in Alternative Lesson Plan Number Two, the responses of the people he interviews. Teachers should, of course, adapt the selection either by substituting a local situation involving an attempt to attract industry to their own locality or by prefacing the question with "If you were a Staten Islander, how would you answer the following questions?"

AN INDUSTRIAL PARK FOR STATEN ISLAND

Staten Island, or Richmond Borough (its official designation), is the most rural of New York City's five boroughs.[3] Wooded hills, pleasant valleys, lakes, streams, and a natural "greenbelt" characterize its landscape. Staten Islanders like their shaded streets, beautiful trees, lovely lawns, flowers and shrubs, and their unhurried way of life, and

[3] The author is indebted for the format of this case study to Richard S. Martin and Reuban G. Miller, *Economics and Its Significance*. Columbus, Ohio, Charles E. Merrill, Inc., 1965.

would like to keep Staten Island that way—with a few improvements of course! Visitors to New York City enjoy the famous five-cent ferry ride across the bay unless they come within whiffing distance of garbage scows on their way to the city dump at the Fresh Kills Landfill Operation. Within a few years, this noxious section of Staten Island, which borders the Arthur Kill—the narrow, polluted body of water which separates it from the fumes and bustle of industrial New Jersey—will be ready for development into an industrial park. While most Staten Islanders anticipate that an influx of industry will raise Staten Island's high living standards still higher, there is disagreement as to how this project should be handled financially and in the best interests of the community.

Alternative A: Should the industrial park be developed by Richmond Borough with a specific bond issue for the project charged as a special assessment against the residents? (Under this arrangement, Staten Islanders would retain control over the nature of the industrial park and its development.)

Alternative B: Should New York City as a whole build the park with municipal funds secured through the sale of bonds? (This would place decision-making in the hands of the Mayor and the Council, in which Richmond Borough has a very weak voice.)

Alternative C: Should the funds be obtained from the state or national government under a matching-funds arrangement? (Such aid would probably come with state or federal strings attached.)

Alternative D: Should a public agency such as the bi-state New York Port Authority, take over the problem of development? (Since New Jersey has an equal voice with New York State on this bi-state commission, this might influence both the rate and the extent of the park's development.)

Alternative E: Should the land be sold or leased to a development corporation as a private venture? (While such an arrangement would remove worries about increased taxes, the community might lose much of its control over its own destiny.)

QUESTIONS:
1. How do you think Staten Island's industrial park project should be handled?
2. Why do you think the alternative which you have chosen is in the best interests of the people of Staten Island?
3. What difficulties do you foresee if your plan is adopted?
4. Which, if any, of the four alternative plans would you also accept? Why?
5. Which of the alternatives, if any, would you vigorously oppose? Why?

Two Alternative Lesson Plans for Teaching the Case Study

The first lesson plan—an informal discussion of the problems raised by building an industrial park on Staten Island—involves the following steps.

First, request the students to read the selection and the alternative solutions to the problems that it poses. Make sure that the facts in the case study are understood by all.

Second, ask the boys and girls to jot down their own answers to the five questions it raises.

Third, start the discussion by asking several students to read their own answers to the class.

Fourth, during the discussion phase of the lesson, make sure that each issue is clarified and understood by all, that all points of view are given a fair hearing, and that the approach to the problem is rational rather than emotional.

Finally, summarize your lesson by polling the class on each issue. In the decision-making phase, the class should grapple with the question of which policy is best and why. There is no need for the class to reach a consensus.

The first lesson plan is useful for teaching or reviewing several economic concepts and issues: the ever-present question of opportunity costs; the advantages and disadvantages of government participation in economic life (how much and at what cost); the use of economic analysis in decision-making, and questions of "values" in economic life (economic progress versus the quality of life in a suburban community).

The second lesson plan requires a more structured approach to the case study. It involves the following steps.

First, request the students to read the selection and the alternative solutions to it. Clarify the facts and the issues involved in the problem.

Second, ask volunteers as an assignment to interview local residents using the five questions. In order to obtain a variety of responses, suggest that the following be included: a parent, a grandparent, a shop keeper, a local manufacturer (if available), an "old" Staten Islander, and a newcomer to Staten Island.

Third, tabulate the responses in class and have them discussed, evaluated, and appraised by a panel of budding "experts" in economic analysis.

Finally, as in lesson one, *poll* the class.

As an alternative to the panel, a guest speaker, possibly a member of the Staten Island Chamber of Commerce, could be invited to present his solution to the problem. Questions from the class would both enliven the lesson and bring alternative solutions before the group. After hearing the arguments and reviewing the evidence, each student should be asked to write an analytical position paper on one of the five alternative solutions to the problem posed in the case study.

Values of Case Studies

Primarily an inductive method of teaching, the case-study method of instruction is valuable on the high school level for several reasons.

1. Interest is immediately aroused because students are discussing real-life problems. The best case studies are built around problems that deal with issues that are immediate, controversial, and worth getting concerned about; and about which something can be done.

2. The student learns by doing. Under the teacher's guidance, he is an active, not a passive participant in the learning process. In fast-changing times, the teacher must provide experiences that will help young people develop the kinds of skills, attitudes, habits of mind, and knowledge that will encourage continuous growth in an ever-changing society. In short, the case-study method enables the student to grow in understanding.

3. The student will learn that there are no quick and easy solutions to persistent economic problems. But the student will use and become familiar with ways of attacking modern problems. And, he may even learn the rudiments of model building.

Gerald Leinwand cautions us, however, that, while case studies are useful and appropriate learning experiences, to structure an entire twelfth-grade one-semester economics course, or the whole K–12 social studies curriculum, on the case-study approach alone "is to fragmatize rather than unify the learning experience of the student." [4]

4 Gerald Leinwand, "Queries on Inquiry in the Social Studies," *Social Education,* 30:413–414 (October 1966).

CHAPTER

11 *Making Economics Come Alive—Related Student Activities*

New Techniques and Approaches

Each generation shapes education to meet the challenges of the times. The present generation has evidenced a deep concern for the intellectual content and the quality of the education that our children are receiving. Students today are presented more and more with source material and raw data and encouraged to discover generalizations for themselves, building one generalization or concept on another until eventually they develop, through the process of inquiry and discovery, the basic structure of the subject they are studying.

Some economics teachers seek out up-to-date economics textbooks that make provision for the wider aims of modern education by furnishing activities, student projects, readings, and discussion questions at the end of each chapter to implement the new approaches. Instead of using textbooks, other teachers are writing and collecting a vast variety of materials—narrative accounts, analytical articles, case studies, sets of statistics, and collections of cartoons—to be used for launching student thinking. In short, students are being encouraged to organize knowledge for themselves as economists, sociologists, and historians organize it.

Of course, the challenge of teaching economics with a vast array of multiple materials and by a variety of methods is a far cry from tranquil, easy old-style textbook-oriented instruction. But, today's teacher cannot afford to teach his subject in simple, obvious, routine ways, if he expects to capture the excitement, the challenge, and the controversy which make economics a lively intellectual discipline. Instead, he must be conversant with a multiplicity of sources and use a variety of teaching tools and colorful approaches. Students grasp the fundamentals of economics more quickly and easily and acquire an understanding of economic concepts in depth if each principle is explained and illustrated for them in a number of illuminating and interesting ways. The classroom techniques and procedures for making economics come alive described in this chapter are all designed to stimulate active pupil participation and to make economics more functional and realistic. Economics teachers should endeavor to accumulate files of materials and devices which serve as a wide and varied reservoir of teaching procedures and techniques upon which they can draw to interest or enrich instruction for a particular class or for individual students within a class. Some of the related student activities, which are listed and briefly discussed in this chapter, must be set in motion by the teacher. A few are in the nature of term projects. Others are really only suggestions to the teacher for teaching certain aspects of a specific topic.

Writing Activities

Economics teachers can develop the verbal skills of their students in the teaching-learning of economic subject matter in several ways. Writing skills, for example, can be strengthened by written reports connected with the following activities.

1. *Writing essays that express the student's beliefs* on such topics as Why I Want to Join the Peace Corps; Why I Joined CORE; Why I Am Participating in Junior Achievement. Essays such as these have added value because the student must organize his thoughts. The experience helps him to systematize his thinking and to express it formally.

2. Presenting *brief supplementary reports* (*written or oral*) based on pamphlets in the Economic Literacy Series (C.A.S.E.), in the Curriculum Resources Inc. Series, in Public Affairs Pamphlets, the Oxford Series, or on current, often fugitive materials issued by the National Association of Manufacturers, the AFL-CIO, and other point-of-view organizations.

Teachers should confer with students in order to help them plan and develop good reports. They should stand by as resource persons to help students who encounter difficulties. To encourage attention while the report is being delivered and to stimulate participation after the reporter has finished, certain members of the class may be responsible for asking questions of the speaker. The question-and-answer period is usually the liveliest and most worthwhile aspect of the lesson.

3. Preparing a class or department *newspaper*, called *ECO* or the *High School Economist*, edited and mimeographed by the students, but occasionally issued by the teacher. It works best for topics like The Teenager and the Economy, The War on Poverty, and Consumers' Problems. It may even include a humor column of "boners," jokes, and verse involving economics ("Echoes from *Eco*"):

> *Economics I understand.*
> *I'm the supply*
> *She's the demand.*

4. Preparing *book reviews* on selected books. Students will enjoy reading and reporting on *The Jungle, Unsafe at Any Speed, The Worldly Philosophers, The Waste Makers,* or *The Hidden Persuaders.*

5. Giving the students an occasional *take-home examination* requiring thought and analysis, at the conclusion of such topics as economic systems, the promotion of economic growth, and solutions for urban problems.

6. Awarding extra credit for *creative writing*, possibly for the class newspaper (editorials, letters to the editor, interviews, "eyewitness" accounts of the Stock Market Crash of 1929, a day in Adam Smith's lecture hall, an interview with Thomas Malthus).

7. Voluntary extra-credit *expository research term papers* on topics such as Early American Economists, Compulsory Health Insurance, the Revolution of Rising Expectations, the Population Explosion, and the Job Corps, involving simple research, the use of the library, and bibliographies.

8. Voluntary extra-credit *analytical research term papers* for brighter students on Causes of Underdevelopment, Varieties of Communist Economies, and the Negative Income Tax, undertakings involving deeper insights and some training in economic analysis.

9. *A position paper*, two typewritten pages in length or its handwritten equivalent, enables a student to analyze a question or a problem independently. Suitable topics for position papers include: Should Congress enact the negative income tax? Is the "new economics" sound? Should the national debt limit be abandoned? Should the United States give foreign aid to countries friendly with Cuba? Before reaching his conclusion and taking his stand, the student must weigh alternative solutions as carefully as he can. Furthermore, when the position papers of his fellows are read and criticized in class, the student has an opportunity to test his own judgment and his tentative solutions against those of others. It is good practice to assign a position paper on

a current problem early in the course. If the students are to become excited about economics, they must be introduced to the controversial aspects of the discipline almost immediately. Writing position papers involves the student to a greater extent than does filling in the blanks in his workbook, encourages him to rely upon his own inner resources to a greater extent than usual, and makes him better prepared to participate in the ensuing classroom discussion.

Oral Activities

Economics teachers can also use oral activities to develop speaking skills in a variety of ways.

1. *Using interviewing techniques.* Often called a "classroom without walls," interviews are best begun by involving people within the school. Teachers who conduct summer camps or run personal businesses are good prospects for topics such as the benefits and burdens of entrepreneurship, labor problems, and forms of business organization.

2. *Sociodrama,* or spontaneous role playing, can be used in dramatizing a board of directors' meeting, stock market operations in which students play the bear, bull, or lamb, a town council discussing the financing of a community swimming pool, a labor-management collective-bargaining session, or the entire class may be converted into a meeting of the United Pretzel Benders of America contemplating a strike call. The essence of sociodrama is realism. Properly used, it can set the stage for introducing new topics, problems, and even units. It usually arouses vigorous interest, stimulates thinking, and dramatizes issues.

3. *Informal teacher-led discussion* can be used effectively to teach economic understandings and concepts. The controversial nature of economic policies is such that various opinions and viewpoints soon arise. By encouraging students to participate in the discussion and to ask questions, the teacher can help the class to separate erroneous ideas from solid fact. The success of classroom discussion depends largely upon the enthusiasm and skill with which a knowledgeable teacher conducts the discussion. Topics such as the Great Society programs to ameliorate poverty, the advantages and shortcomings of other economic systems such as the Soviet, Swedish, or Indian, and controversial tax proposals before Congress usually arouse a spirited verbal interplay.

4. *Formal discussion* includes roundtables, debates, panels, and the reports of student committees.

In a *roundtable* three to five "authorities" discuss a topic such as causes of and remedies for inflation, the merits of various types of life insurance, or proposed remedies for business cycles. At the close of formal presentations and rebuttals, the audience should be invited to participate.

An occasional *debate* may be held on a current controversial issue, such as a round of tax increases or cuts, or more or less foreign aid for underdeveloped countries that do business with Red China.

Panels, forums, and *town-meeting* discussions under a moderator are suitable for large audiences such as those gathered for assembly programs. The panel technique is a good device for airing the pros and cons of controversial issues. Students enjoy hearing two or more opposing interests fight it out before an interested audience.

Student committees are usually more suited to junior high school than to a twelfth-grade economics course. While committees give students an opportunity to work together and to share information, the process can be an exercise in futility unless both the students and the teacher plan the committees' work carefully and select good group leaders. It can be used occasionally to teach such topics as labor-management relations, government spending and taxation, comparative economic systems, and problems of world trade.

Audio-Visual Aids

Every economics teacher has traditional visual aids available for his use. The *chalkboard* is an old stand-by and should be used for notes, diagrams, and difficult words. Chalkboard presentations, used in explaining new concepts and in outlining and analyzing economic problems, should be carefully planned. Colored crayon, neat arrangements, and legibly written or printed words will make this kind of presentation more effective. In presenting his lesson, the teacher should talk to the class, not to the chalkboard.

1. Educators estimate that 50 percent more material can be presented on the *flannel board* than on the chalkboard in a comparable period of time. Since the props are produced in advance of the lesson, the teacher presents his material while facing the class.

2. Classroom materials such as charts, news clippings, pictures, cartoons, and students' work can be exhibited conveniently and effectively through **bulletin-board displays**. Obviously the exhibits should be current and illustrative of the topic under consideration. While an economics bulletin board should be attractive, the teacher should consider it primarily as a learning tool, not as a display of art.

3. Teachers should, of course, also incorporate in their lessons the attractive *pictures, charts, tables,* and *graphic materials* which appear in modern high school economics textbooks. Illustrated *home-made work sheets* can easily be prepared by using a copier to prepare stencils for the mimeograph or spirit-duplicating machine. Such work sheets may be used by the teacher from time to time to incorporate charts, graphs, statistics, problems, hard-to-find information or an outstanding cartoon.

4. Of course, no teacher should fail to use the *filmstrip* and the *sound film* when and where it is available. Teachers should be familiar with the procedures in their schools for selecting, ordering, presenting, and evaluating a film or filmstrip. If good procedures are followed the audio-visual presentation will be a meaningful learning experience for the students. In general, filmstrips have the advantage of flexibility and can be used at varying rates of speed, stopped for explanations and discussion, and "edited" by skipping frames of little educational or motivational value or not pertinent to the topic under discussion.

A *filmstrip* lesson in economics requires previewing by the teacher and careful planning to help the students to see relationships, to have available stimulating questions, and to determine in advance the frames to be emphasized. The filmstrip may be employed as

An introduction or motivation of a particular unit such as consumers' problems, labor-management relations, or the functions of the banking system

The body of a lesson on a topic such as the effects of automation

A summary after the study of urban economic problems or the farm problem

An overview of future units to be studied by showing strips depicting other economic systems

A review of previous lessons.

The filmstrip lesson may be presented by the teacher or by a student who has previewed the filmstrip and engaged in pre-planning. If a student, or group of students, prepares the script and presents the lesson, adequate provision, as a rule, must be made for a teacher-led summary to derive maximum educational benefit from the experience.

Teachers should use audio-visual materials as aids, not as substitutes for teaching. Select the type that promises to be most useful for your purpose and plan to use it at the most opportune stage of the lesson or unit. Prepare the class by telling the students what to look for, and supplement the frames with explanations and discussion. Check up by using an informal quiz which will clinch the significance of the activity and make its use of value.

The suggestions just given for the use of filmstrips in teaching economics apply, for the most part, to the use of *sound films*. Motion pictures, of course, usually involve students emotionally because they bring them vicariously to "where the action is." Amo De Bernadis has prepared an indispensable aid for the economics teacher who is seeking a suitable film for viewing by his class: *100 Selected Films in Economic Education* (published by the Joint Council on Economic Education) is an annotated list of motion-picture films alphabetically arranged by title. Each annotation includes an indication of the appropriate grade level, suggested areas of the curriculum, a synopsis of the film's coverage, a listing of questions raised by the film, and some suggested activities.

5. The overhead projector and the improved opaque projector equipped with lenses sufficiently powerful to show pictures under conditions of less than total darkness are indispensable teaching tools. The overhead projector enables teachers to face the class while carrying on a discussion. Teachers can use prepared transparencies, including overlays (transparencies placed over the one being projected), or they can produce transparencies in class while teaching by the use of a special wax pencil or a china marker. The opaque projector will project a page of a book, a mounted picture, or a specimen such as a "greenback," all in color, of course. Transparencies, either commercially prepared or home made, can easily be filed away for future use.

6. An alert and enthusiastic economics teacher will also make use of *student-made audio-visual aids and realia* such as coins, corporation reports, stocks, and ticker tape which pupils will often bring to class. Student-made aids include snapshots taken on field trips to industrial plants, tape recordings of television or radio programs, scripts written by students for specific filmstrips, drawings, charts, and cartoons. Students like to present filmstrips themselves, especially if the student is featured as the lecturer for the day or as an expert on, for example, automation. Sound films can often be used as the springboard to class discussion. Examples of interesting sound films include *With These Hands* (ILGWU), the *Federal Reserve System,* and films of commercial and industrial firms. Another rich vein is kinescopes of outstanding television programs and, of course, live commercial and educational television programs.

Some teachers use "Looking and Listening" in *Senior Scholastic* as a guide to worthwhile *television programs* for students. The accounts of the subjects of the features serve as motivation. While the range of programs is wide, topics of direct or peripheral interest to economics classes are often included. Other teachers reserve a place on their chalkboard or bulletin board for "Coming T.V. Attractions," offer extra credit for viewing the television feature, and conduct a brief discussion or ask their students to submit brief written reports on it the next day. Of course, events such as the President's Economic Report, his Budget Message, and his State of the Union Message warrant more extended treatment. If a debate on an economic issue is part of a political campaign, students should be encouraged to use their critical faculties and analytical powers not only to verify factual data but also to analyze the speaker's appeal, to examine his assumptions, and to ferret out bromides of the conventional wisdom his speech may contain.

Demonstrations

A teacher can develop visually all of the functions of the modern commercial bank by showing the origin of banks during the Middle Ages. Using bags of round cheese wafers to simulate golden ducats, he can demonstrate how the medieval goldsmith—the prototype of the modern banker—discovered the laws of probability of withdrawals, the principles of the clearing house, and the convenience of using bank notes. A demonstration such as this is an excellent way to introduce the principles of banking, a topic which the teacher often finds difficult to explain.

Interpretation of Graphic Materials

Sir William Petty, a seventeenth-century British economist, asserted that information expressed "in terms of Number, Weight, and Measure" was superior to the adjectives of ordinary speech. Economics teachers agree that tables, charts, and graphs are worth thousands of words.

Cartoons, posters, graphs, tables, charts, and diagrams are extremely valuable for presenting economic concepts and data to students in easily understood form. Among the activities that a teacher can suggest to develop these skills are:

1. Constructing *flow charts* (from iron ore to finished steel)
2. Depicting GNP, NI, and the Cost of Living Index in *graphic form*
3. Selecting the *economic cartoon of the week* for display on the bulletin board
4. Drawing an *organizational chart* for a corporation

Simple charts, constructed by students, can be prepared from data based on *Road Maps for Industry, The New York Times, U.S. News & World Report, Newsweek,* and so on. Graphic material collected or constructed by the students should be exhibited on the economics bulletin board. It is a good idea to have a single theme for each exhibit, for example, the President's Economic Report, automation, or a collection of cartoons on economic topics.

Field Trips

Individual or class visits to local manufacturing plants provide first-hand experience and deeper insights and add realism to economic study. A well-planned field trip enables the student to see the economic world in action. If your school is near a large city, the class might visit a stock exchange, a large bank, or a newspaper plant. The success of a class trip depends on the degree of planning. Planning includes making complete arrangements in advance on a specific time schedule, formulating the purpose of the trip with advance preparation of logical questions to which answers will be sought during the trip, selecting group leaders, and appointing committees responsible for special aspects of the trip such as transportation, safety, and courtesy. Every trip should be evaluated and a record should be kept of it by collecting samples, brochures, snapshots, and possibly even making a motion picture of some of the operations. Each trip should be followed by an analysis and discussion in the classroom and by a thank-you note to the host. Often an effective field trip can be followed up by inviting a speaker to discuss the work of the bank, factory, or government agency just visited. The local Social Security office will be pleased, as a rule, to send a speaker with a motion-picture film to your own classroom to discuss aspects of social security. Often seeing economics in action makes the content of the textbook more practical and encourages students to do economics assignments conscientiously.

The Stock-Market Game

Teachers have long used variations on the so-called stock-market game.

1. One version of the stock-market game involves the imaginary investment of a sum of money ($1,000) in securities, buying and selling for a definite pre-arranged period, and keeping a record of gains and losses by using the stock-market quotations. The teacher awards a prize to the student who has made the most money.

2. Another version involves the actual purchase of a share of stock by

the class. This makes each member of the class a capitalist with a share in our economy. The stock can be donated to some worthy cause at the end of the school year.

Teaching about the securities market by having students follow the stock-market quotations on a share of stock which the class has purchased is to provide a practical experience in economic analysis. Have the students buy a share in the largest corporation of their community so that they can study the role of their company in the local economy. If it is possible for the students to attend an annual shareholders meeting, their sense of participation will be enhanced. Not only will the students understand more clearly how their corporation affects the community's economic development, and how, in turn, their corporation is affected by the development of the community, but they will also find out how their local corporation relates to the national economy. Many of the analytical tools of the economist can be introduced into the unit, and the students will thus learn through personal experience how economic analysis can help them to understand matters which are of importance to them.

Teachers can also use other simple games. Write a stock-market quotation on the blackboard. Let each student pick a card on which is indicated the role he is to play in the market (bull, bear, speculator, investor). Each student goes to the front of the room to explain what he would do in the light of the information given in the quotation. This game can be applied to such persons as the receiver of a pension, a day laborer, a hardware dealer, when there is a sudden rise or fall in prices.

Materials File

A beginning teacher should start at least two files early in his teaching career:

1. A *test questions file*, described in a later chapter
2. A *materials file*

A materials file enables a teacher to find and to use the articles, pictures, cartoons, diagrams, and graphs, which all teachers hoard but cannot find when they need them most. Teacher-discovered materials stimulate better teaching. There are five main steps in creating a materials file.

1. Obtain folders or an accordion file for clippings, pictures, small pamphlets.
2. Find a place to store your materials. A filing cabinet is ideal, but paper boxes stored in a closet will do.

3. Start a filing system with folder tabs, preferably by topic or subject.
4. Make an index (a sheet or two).
5. Make notations for cross-references.

Team Teaching

The purpose of team teaching in high school economics is to utilize the teachers' special skills, areas of interest, and abilities, thereby enriching the students' education through a variety of experiences. Team teaching encourages the mutual sharing of ideas and materials and makes possible both large- and small-group instruction. While one member of the team is lecturing or conducting a large-scale activity, the other members can work with small groups. Team teaching can be especially useful for beginners because it enables them to observe experienced master teachers in operation. Teachers are freer to plan, to study, to be creative, or to relax. On the other hand, team teaching has serious shortcomings. Not all teachers are prepared either academically or psychologically to emerge from their isolated classroom kingdoms to abandon individualism and to work cooperatively with their colleagues. Moreover, economics probably requires more tutorial assistance from the individual teacher than the team-teacher situation may allow. Further, some schools do not have the space for both large- and small-group instruction. Finally, team teaching works best with motivated, attentive, well-behaved middle-class students. The lecture method has never been notably successful with pupils of lesser ability or motivation.

Teachers interested in the team-teaching approach will profit by reading "A One Year Course in Economics Utilizing Team Teaching and Elective Units" (Donald B. Johnstone, *Economic Education Experiences of Enterprising Teachers,* Vol. IV, 1967, pp. 38–39) and "Team Teaching: Let's Look Before We Leap!" (Jack R. Fraenkel and Richard E. Gross, *Social Education,* **30**:335–337, May 1966).

Games and Simulation

In the real world, games and simulation are being used more and more by business and the military as training devices. In the world of the high school classroom, games provide both the usual enjoyment of playing games and genuine learning experiences. Teachers who are interested in reading about the possibilities of using games to teach economics can read about two grade-six games: "Sierra Leone Development Project," simulating the economic problems of an emerging nation, and "The Free Enterprise Game," simulating the role of the owner of a toy store (Leonard W. Ingraham, "Teachers, Computers, and Games: Innovations in the Social Studies," *Social Education*, 31:51–53, January 1967). "A Game for Teaching Foreign Trade in Twelfth Grade" (Dennis W. Cambier, *Economic Education Experiences of Enterprising Teachers*, Vol. IV, 1967, pp. 38–39) provides another worthwhile learning experience.

Programmed Instruction

Programmed instruction in economics consists of "an attempt to approximate without a live teacher certain critical features of good tutorial instruction." The salient feature of good tutorial instruction is continual interchange of ideas between pupil and teacher and immediate feedback so that the student always knows whether his response is correct. Programmed instruction is simple, logical, sequential step-by-step instruction involving self-teaching through the use of specially developed texts. Each successive step builds upon the preceding, progressing from simple to complex, until the student can perform complicated skills and solve difficult problems. Obviously the programmer must know in advance exactly what he wants to teach. The material to be programmed is then broken down into small, easily absorbed units called *frames*. Usually an economics program is a bulky book consisting of a large number of frames which may total one thousand or more. A teaching machine is merely a device for presenting the frames more conveniently for the viewer.

The Behavioral Research Laboratories (Ladera Professional Center, Box 577, Palo Alto, California) has produced a series of programmed textbooks for teaching high school economics. *The American Economics Series* includes:

Richard E. Attiyeh, *Capitalism, Communism, and Socialism*
Richard E. Attiyeh, *Problems of Economic Stability and Growth*
Richard E. Attiyeh, *Taxes and Government Spending*
Keith G. Lumsden, *The Free Enterprise System*
Keith G. Lumsden, *The Gross National Product*
Keith G. Lumsden, *International Trade*
Samuel Weiner, *The Federal Reserve System and Its Effect on Money and Banking*
A Teacher's Manual and a Test Booklet are available with each text.

Leonard W. Ingraham, Chairman of the Programmed Instruction Committee of the National Council for the Social Studies, points out that two dangers seem to be inherent in programmed instruction: excessive commercialization and "educational sclerosis"—a lack of imagination in presenting the materials. Current programs and programmed instruction do not stimulate curiosity or the spirit of discovery. Instead, they concentrate solely upon the imparting of knowledge. Dr. Ingraham cautions that we are dealing with immature technology. Since the appearance of a program is sometimes deceptive, sound advice still is: "Never judge a program by its title!" [1]

Resources for Teachers

Chapter 15, "Additional Reading and Study Materials and Teacher Aids," provides a comprehensive treatment of the subject. In this section, a few of these aids will be described because they are so closely allied to the related activities just discussed.

The most useful resource manual is still *Teaching Economics* (New York State Department of Education, August 1962). Edited by Albert Alexander, Executive Director of the New York City Council on Economic Education, the handbook, designed to be used to supplement materials studied in problems of democracy and in American history, as well as in economics, cuts across all high school social studies curricula. Because of the inherent complexity of much of the subject matter of economics, emphasis was placed on the upper-grade levels. A resource book rather than a methods book or course of study, *Teaching Economics* provides related student activities on ten topics: the American Economic System, Resources and Economic Growth, the Economics of Business Enterprise, the Economics of Agriculture, the Economics of Labor-Management Relations, Family and Personal Economics, Economic Stabilization, Public Finance, the Money, Credit, and Banking System, and the United States and International Economics. The ten topics were selected for teachability rather than for inclusiveness and specialization. *Teaching Economics* contains a bibliography useful for general reference and for enrichment, and an address list for sources of free and inexpensive pamphlet materials. It is helpful to teachers in planning interesting and realistic classroom procedures for economic understanding and is a useful supplement in all classes which explore economic areas and activities.

In the field of teaching materials, Laurence E. Leamer and Percy L. Guyton, *Suggestions for a Basic Economics Library* (New York, Joint

[1] Leonard W. Ingraham, "Programmed Instructional Materials in Social Studies: 1964," *Social Education,* 29:27–28 (January 1965).

Council on Economic Education, 1965) consists of an annotated bibliography including the works of 240 authors, which is designed to guide, step by step, the building of an economics library for the school, the classroom, or the individual. Jere W. Clark and Percy L. Guyton (eds.), *Economic Education Experiences of Enterprising Teachers* (New York, Joint Council on Economic Education, Vol. 1, 1963; Vol. 2, 1965; Vol. 3, 1966; Vol. 4, 1967, George G. Dawson [ed.]) contains the prize-winning entries in the Kazanjian Foundation Awards Program for the Teaching of Economics. In addition, some five hundred teacher-made projects, collected since the inception of the Awards Program in 1962, are available to teachers on request without fee through the inter-library loan system from the New York University Center for Economic Education, which serves as a depository for the Kazanjian Collection.

The Joint Council on Economic Education publishes a variety of materials on the secondary school level. A useful guide for teachers and curriculum designers is Julian C. Aldrich's *How to Construct and Use a Resource Unit* (New York, Joint Council on Economic Education, 1964). "Invaluable resource units" is the phrase that best describes the Joint Council's *Economic Topics* (New York, Joint Council on Economic Education, 1963, 1964, 1966), a collection of articles from the Joint Council's *Newsletter* on vital economic topics by leading economists and articles by outstanding teachers suggesting ways of teaching such problems as inflation, growth, and income distribution.

The Task Force

After the Task Force issued its report, economists turned their attention to developing materials. Encouraged by the Joint Council on Economic Education, they organized a number of centers in colleges and school systems around the country where writers develop materials and try them out in elementary and secondary school classes. For these groups, the Council published *Teacher's Guide to Developmental Economic Education Program* (New York, 1964): Part One, *Economic Ideas and Concepts—Based on the Task Force Report,* by James D. Calderwood, is implemented by Part Two, *Suggestions for Grade Placement and Development of Economic Ideas and Concepts.* Part One consists of elaborations upon the meanings and implications of the main economic ideas and concepts in the Task Force report. Part Two is the result of a conference of four groups of specialists who undertook to provide samples of how the leading economic ideas and concepts can be introduced into the school system at different grade levels and in various courses.

Harlan Smith's *Study Guide for Selected Sixty-Session Series of the American Economy TV Films* (New York, Joint Council on Economic Education, 1964) is primarily for teachers using the films selected by John R. Coleman as the core of the television course first taught in 1962–1963. The guide briefly summarizes the content of each film, identifies the key ideas, suggests effective ways of using each film, gives sample questions and problems to stimulate interest and discussion, offers some testing suggestions, and lists references.

Economics and the Consumer (New York, Joint Council on Economic Education, 1966) presents in detail the principles of economics through experiences of the student and his family. The booklet identifies and elaborates upon the minimum understanding which high school graduates need to make wise decisions as consumers. The booklet is a basis for in-service programs, and gives suggestions for the production of materials and the development of scope and sequence over a wide range of high school curricula.

Recent High School Textbooks

How does a teacher select the textbook for his class? Only the teacher himself can supply the answer. The textbook that is best for your class depends upon your aims, the scope and sequence of the course, and the abilities, needs, and interests of your students. A teacher should ask the following questions concerning a textbook before he adopts it for class use.

CHECKLIST FOR EXAMINING A TEXTBOOK
1. Does the content of the textbook promote the aims of the course?
2. Is the content adaptable to an analytical approach, or is it mainly institutional, and personal-problems-oriented?
3. Is the text geared to the reading, maturity, and ability levels of the students?
4. Is the scholarship sound and up-to-date?
5. Do the authors have the training, teaching experience, and viewpoint necessary to produce a teachable textbook on the high school level?
6. Is its content practical, related to the real-life experiences of the boys and girls, and challenging to teen-agers?
7. Is the textbook well-organized, concrete, and written in a vivid, interesting style?
8. Are the physical aspects of the book (size, strength of binding, format, type, and index) satisfactory?

9. Are its teaching and learning aids—graphs, charts, tables, pictures, diagrams, questions, and related student activities—helpful?
10. Is the textbook a part of a "package" consisting of a well-written teacher's manual, a useful students' workbook, tests and examinations, and possibly audiovisual aids such as filmstrips?

The Center for Economic Education, New York University, has prepared *A Description of High School Economics Textbooks* (New York, 1965) designed to provide facts for teachers who ask, "What textbook should I use?" Of the dozen economics textbooks now in use, the following best reflect the influence of the Task Force Report and the impact of the current drive to make high school economics more analytical and less descriptive in nature.

Alexander, Albert, Edward C. Prehn, and Arnold W. Sametz, *The Modern Economy in Action: An Analytical Approach.* New York: Pitman Publishing Corporation, 1968.

Calderwood, James D., and George L. Fersh, *Economics in Action.* New York: Macmillan, 1968.

Gordon, Sanford D., and Jess Witchell, *An Introduction to the American Economy: Analysis and Policy.* Boston: D. C. Heath and Company, 1967.

Lindholm, Richard W., and Paul Driscoll, *Our American Economy.* New York: Harcourt, Brace and World, Inc., 1964.

Mortenson, William P., Donald T. Krider, and Roy J. Sampson, *Understanding Our Economy: Analysis-Issues-Principles.* Boston: Houghton Mifflin Company, 1964.

Wronski, Stanley P., Francis S. Doody, and Richard V. Clemence, *Modern Economics.* Boston: Allyn and Bacon, Inc., 1964.

Supplementary Readings for High School Students

The curriculum revolution in economics produced a variety of short paperback books to supply the new demand for challenging, interesting, meaningful materials. The following booklets, pamphlets, and books are intended specifically for high school use:

The series *Studies in Economic Issues* (Scott, Foresman and Company) includes the following titles.

Boylan, Myles, *Economics of the Community.* 111 pp.

Calderwood, James D., *International Economic Problems.* 71 pp.

Calderwood, James D., and Hazel J. Jones, *World Trade.* 68 pp.

Daugherty, Marion, *Understanding Economic Growth.* 119 pp.

Lovenstein, Meno, *Capitalism, Communism, Socialism.* 150 pp.

Senesh, Lawrence, and Barbara Warne Newell, *Our Labor Force.* 84 pp.

The series *Area Studies in Economic Progress* (Scott, Foresman and Company) includes the following booklets.

Babian, Haig, *The Middle East—Old Problems and New Hopes.* 76 pp.

Berkowitz, Monroe, *India—Struggle Against Time.* 72 pp.

Calderwood, James D., *Western Europe and the Common Market.* 72 pp.

Chang, Perry Peng, *China—Development by Force.* 80 pp.

Hunsberger, Warren S., *Japan—Lessons in Enterprise.* 72 pp.

Madden, Carl, *Latin America—Reform or Revolution.* 72 pp.

Salkever, Louis R., and Helen M. Flynn, *Sub-Saharan Africa—Struggle Against the Past.* 72 pp.

Schwartz, Harry, *The Soviet Union—Communist Economic Power.* 72 pp.

A Teacher's Manual is available with this series.

The series *Economic Forces in American History* (Scott, Foresman and Company) includes the following booklets.

Robert E. Gallman, *Developing the American Colonies, 1607–1783.* 64 pp.

Douglass C. North, *Decisions That Faced the Nation, 1783–1820.* 72 pp.

William N. Parker, *Commerce, Cotton, and Westward Expansion, 1820–1860.* 72 pp.

Lance E. Davis, *Growth of Industrial Enterprise, 1860–1914.* 72 pp.

Duncan McDougall, *World Power and New Problems, 1914–1930.* 64 pp.

Eugene Smolensky, *Adjustments to Depression and War, 1930–1945.* 72 pp.

Haig Babian, *Problems of Prosperity and Leadership, 1945–   .* 80 pp.

A Teacher's Guidebook is also available with this series.

The *American Problems Series* (Holt, Rinehart and Winston) is designed to accompany the textbook *Problems of Democracy: The United States in a Changing World,* by Edna and Herbert Bohlman and includes the following booklets.

Feinberg, Daniel, *Consumer Economics.* 94 pp.

Goldstein, Bernard, and Harry Stark, *Entering the Labor Force.* 96 pp.

Kreps, Juanita M., *Automation and Employment.* 78 pp.

Kreps, Juanita M., *Taxation, Spending, and the National Debt.* 64 pp.

Robinson, Warren C., *Economic Growth.* 80 pp.

The *C.A.S.E. Economic Literacy Series* (McGraw-Hill) includes the following titles.

de Rycke, Laurence (ed.), *Beginning Readings in Economics.* 384 pp.

de Rycke, Laurence, and Alvin H. Thompson, *Business Enterprise in the American Economy.* 124 pp.

Leamer, Laurence E., and Dorothy L. Thompson, *American Capitalism: An Introduction.* 128 pp.

Lee, Baldwin, *Capitalism and Other Economic Systems.* 132 pp.

Steinberg, David J., *The U.S.A. in the World Economy.* 120 pp.

Welfing, Weldon, *Money and Banking in the American Economy.* 112 pp.

Teacher's Manuals are available for each title.

The Oxford Book Company includes a number of economics pamphlets and unit texts in its publications. Among the most useful titles are:

Korey, Edward L., *Business and the American Way*

Pruden, Durwood, *Democracy, Capitalism and Their Competitors*

Starr, Mark, *Labor and the American Way*

Public Affairs Pamphlets (381 Park Avenue South, New York 10016) offers numerous titles on social and economic problems. Convenient, concise, and interesting, the booklets serve as excellent sources for oral and written reports on consumers' problems, medicare, social security, the balance of payments, the labor movement in the United States, the war on poverty and a host of other timely topics.

Nontextbook Reading Materials

Although the class textbook remains the common core of the high school economics course, some teachers use a variety of nontextbook reading materials. In general, such types of reading fall under six headings.

1. *Biographies*

Biographies of economists, captains of industry, union leaders, and even dreamers like Edward Bellamy. Perhaps the most useful book in this category is Robert L. Heilbroner's *Worldly Philosophers.*

2. *Specialized Accounts*

Allen, Frederick Lewis, *The Big Change: America Transforms Itself, 1900–1950.* New York, Bantam Books, 1965.

Campbell, Robert W., *Soviet Economic Power.* New York, Houghton Mifflin Company, 1960.

Galbraith, John Kenneth, *The Affluent Society*. New York, Houghton
　Mifflin Company, 1958.
Galbraith, John Kenneth, *The New Industrial State*. New York,
　Houghton Mifflin Company, 1967.
Heilbroner, Robert L., *The Making of Economic Society*. Englewood
　Cliffs, New Jersey, Prentice-Hall, Inc., 1962.
Packard, Vance, *The Waste Makers*. New York, David McKay, Inc.,
　1960.
Whyte, W. H. Jr., *The Organization Man*. New York, Simon and
　Schuster, 1956.

3. *Imaginative Literature*

Steinbeck's *Grapes of Wrath*, Upton Sinclair's *Jungle*, and other
muckraking novels of the early twentieth century come under this head-
ing.

4. *Source Books of Readings*

Ammer, Dean S., *Readings and Cases in Economics*. Boston, Ginn and
　Company, 1966.
de Rycke, Laurence (ed.), *Beginning Readings in Economics*. New
　York, McGraw-Hill, 1962.

5. *Reference Books*

Reference works are described in Chapter 15, "Additional Reading
and Study Materials and Teacher Aids." In brief, government publications, pamphlets issued by labor, industrial, and farm organizations, and
college textbooks are perhaps the most useful on the high school level.
College textbooks today are really economics encyclopedias. In fact,
they provide the high school teacher with a useful means of keeping
only one or two steps behind new developments in the discipline.
Among the most useful college textbooks for background for a teacher
of the one-semester twelfth-grade economics course are the following.

Bach, George L., *Economics: An Introduction to Analysis and Policy*,
　6th ed. Englewood Cliffs, New Jersey, Prentice-Hall, Inc., 1968.
Bye, Richard T., and William W. Hewett, *The Economic Process: Its
　Principles and Problems*. New York, Appleton-Century-Crofts, 1963.
Harriss, C. Lowell, *The American Economy: Principles, Practices and
　Policies*. Homewood, Illinois, Richard D. Irwin, Inc., 1962.
Homan, Paul T., Albert G. Hart, and William W. Sametz, *The Eco-*

nomic Order: An Introduction to Theory and Policy. New York, Harcourt, Brace and World, Inc., 1958.

Samuelson, Paul A., *Economics: An Introductory Analysis.* New York, McGraw-Hill, 1964.

Villard, Henry H., *Economic Performance: An Introduction to Economics.* New York, Holt, Rinehart and Winston, Inc., 1961.

6. *Fugitive Materials*

Fugitive materials are the pamphlets, leaflets, and tracts issued by labor organizations, consumer groups, industrial groups, and foundations. Often clever and controversial, they usually spark discussion in a lively economics class and can be used in propaganda analysis and the application of analytical thinking.

CHAPTER

12 *Consumer Economics in the One-Semester High School Economics Course*

The Need for Consumer Education

Formal education for consumers in American schools first began in home economics courses. The need of the average American to get his money's worth during the depression of the 1930's enabled the advocates of consumer education to establish beachheads in a variety of courses—economics, economic citizenship, problems of democracy, homemaking, and business subjects. Leading educators of the day stated that any knowledge which helps consumers spend their money more wisely is valid economic education on the secondary school level. Forty years ago, Henry Harap, a pioneer in consumer education, said, "Day by day, the great mass of people are blundering in their daily habits of consumption." [1] Young married couples, and some older ones as well, experience unhappiness largely because of poor money management, that is, failure to budget sensibly and to live within their means. Much advertising gives consumers a false sense of values about automobiles, cosmetics, food, clothing, and household appliances. For reasons like these, many economics and business-education teachers strongly advocate that management of personal finances should be among the topics covered in economic education. In their view, any

[1] Henry Harap, *Economic Life and the Curriculum.* New York, The Macmillan Company, 1927, p. 29.

educational experience that contributes to the economic competence of the individual as a consumer, wage earner, saver, investor, or taxpayer is a kind of economic education. Only if the schools teach the American people to lead effective economic lives will they cast their nickel, dime, and dollar votes for beauty, comfort, and health.

The twenty-five million teen-agers in the United States today spend about $15 billion a year. This amounts to approximately $625 per teen-ager annually, not including the money that parents ordinarily spend for their support. In this age of teen-age affluence, your students have already accumulated an infinite variety of consumer goods through gifts and their own purchases. Most television commercials are beamed in their direction, both because teen-agers are carefree spenders now and because they will be the adult market of the future. Jean Baer, senior editor of *Seventeen,* recently told a meeting of the Soap and Detergent Association,

Catch a teen-age girl and put her in your pocket now and you'll keep her forever. Now's the time to sew her up—before the rice is in her hair, before the stork is on the roof, before the wolf is at the door. Set her textured stockings on the path to your product now—and she'll come back blindfolded, baby-strollered, and, one day, bifocaled.[2]

It is for reasons such as these that Dr. James E. Mendenhall, Educational Director of Consumers Union, thinks that consumer education is indispensable to help the consumers become prudent managers of their personal and family finances; wise buyers of goods and services in the marketplace; careful users of personal and public possessions; and informed and intelligent-acting consumer citizens.[3] Consumer education makes two main assumptions: first, that consumers want to improve their status, and, second, that the chief obstacles to improved status have been ignorance, unscrupulous selling tactics, and government agencies financially and politically handicapped in their efforts to aid the consumer. In three decades of finger-pointing, rarely has the consumer pointed his finger at himself. Few efforts have aimed at self-analysis of consumer faults that hurt the consumer as a buyer and a borrower. Perhaps future consumer education courses should use "a big mirror as a teaching aid." [4]

[2] Jean Baer, "The Teenage Consumer," *Aerosol Age* (March 1967), p. 29.
[3] James E. Mendenhall, "Youth Needs and School Responsibilities," *The Bulletin of the National Association of Secondary School Principals* (October 1967), p. 18.
[4] Edward Damon, "Consumer Education Rides Again," *The Clearing House,* 40:391–396 (March 1966).

Consumer Education versus Consumer Economics

The impetus of the Great Depression resulted in a growth in consumer education that lasted a quarter of a century, reaching its peak in the middle of the 1950's before being rolled back by the affluent society and the drive for more academic content after the advent of Sputnik. About a decade ago, the heavy emphasis on consumer economics and the personal problems approach in the one-semester high school course in economics came under heavy attack. The economics profession was appalled by the lack of attention given in the high school course to models, structure, and the analytical tools of the economist.

For example, in 1960 the Textbook Committee of the American Economic Association stated that it found that high school textbooks generally attempt to portray economics as a part of life and to make it appealing to teen-agers on personal grounds; however, the committee claimed that "the space given to consumer economics is out of balance" and that personal economic problems are stressed at the expense of analysis, studies in depth, macroeconomics, nonprice competition, the role of technology, urbanization, and the concept of welfare. Consumer economics received another setback in 1961 with the National Task Force Report, *Economic Education in the Schools*, which emphasized the economic principles that a citizen must know for wise decision-making as a voter rather than his personal problems as a consumer.

Consumer education and consumer economics are not synonymous. *Consumer education* treats descriptively such topics as how to budget income, how to use credit, how to get your money's worth, how to buy life insurance, and how to obtain a social security card. *Consumer economics*, on the other hand, involves the technique of thinking rationally about such things as alternate uses of limited income, the effects of price changes, imperfect competition, and government regulation on the art of buymanship. An analytical lesson must never be just a lesson on "how to buy an automobile" but a lesson on "how to buy anything," using the buying of an automobile as an illustration but emphasizing rational behavior in all situations involving the purchase of a durable good. The professional economist believes that, after a consumer's problem has been analyzed from the point of view of personal economics, the problem must be generalized to demonstrate its socio-economic implications. In other words, according to the professional economist, consumer education is not economics in the broad sense of the term because economics as a discipline is interested in structure, conceptual framework, basic principles, and the tools of the economist, and is not concerned with the transitory details of the art of spending, better techniques of purchasing, and the development of consumer skills in the market.

On no other issue in economic education are the views of the professional economist and the high school teacher of economics so far apart as on the role of consumer education in secondary school economics. In 1965, for example, the New York University Center for Economic Education revealed that New York City's high school teachers lean heavily toward descriptive, personalized, consumer-oriented economics, while the college economists strongly favor analytical principles for high school classes. Using all high school textbooks then in print and eight of the best-selling college Principles of Economics texts, Professor George G. Dawson listed forty topics which are typically included in high school and in introductory college courses. The list was sent to high school teachers of economics and to the college economists involved in the economic education movement. These two groups agreed strongly on only *four* of the forty items. For example, the topic of labor ranked first in popularity with the high school teachers, but only fourteenth with the college economists. Consumers problems ranked second with the high school group, but nineteenth with the college group. Welfare and Social Security placed fifth with the high school people, but a lowly thirtieth with college teachers.

Economics and the Consumer

An attempt to restore consumer economics to its rightful place in the high school course was the publication in 1966 of *Economics and the Consumer*, a Joint Council on Economic Education report by the members of the National Commission on Economics and the Consumer. In the Preface to this forty-page pamphlet, which attempts to show high school teachers how to develop competence in personal decision-making, Dr. M. L. Frankel, President of the JCEE, points out that the Task Force Report did not spell out in detail the principles of economics needed for wise decision-making by the consumer acting independently as a householder. Nor did the Task Force underscore the intimate relationship—indeed the frequent identity—of the principles of economics that must be understood by the consumer as he acts collectively through the ballot box and those principles which he must understand when he acts independently as a buyer, saver, borrower, and investor. *Economics and the Consumer* attempts to identify the basic principles of consumer economics and apply them to situations which confront the consumer in his role as buyer, saver, borrower, investor, and voter.

Although *Economics and the Consumer* should be applauded as an attempt to overcome the reluctance of the professional economist to consider consumer education as economics, it has, in the opinion of many teachers and leaders in the field of consumer education, failed in its effort to right the balance and to bridge the gap between consumer education and economics as an academic discipline. While its economics is impeccable, *Economics and the Consumer* does not paint an adequate or realistic picture of the facts of economic life as encountered by the consumer in his home, in the market place, and in his relation with the government. Its sins are sins of omission rather than of commission. It slights consumer-credit problems, fair trade laws, food and drug laws, grade-labeling controversies, high-pressure brand name salesmanship, the substitution of paper-enclosed air for package contents, and the establishment of standards of quality, safety, and efficiency for consumer goods. It omits the names of such independent, nonprofit, noncommercial membership organizations as the Consumers Union which has been interested in consumer education since 1936, and the names of such consumer-interest government agencies as the Food and Drug Administration, the Federal Trade Commission, the Social Security Administration, the Federal Communications Commission, the Treasury Department, and the President's Committee on Consumer Interests, headed by Betty Furness, Special Assistant to the President for Consumer Affairs. In short, it fails to come to grips with many of the most pressing problems of consumers and fails to contribute substantially to the curricular resources in this vital area. Nevertheless, *Economics and the Consumer* does highlight the idea of integrating consumer education with analytical economics, and it is this idea that economists and educators must continue to develop.

Consumer Education: The First Surge

During its first two decades, the depression-ridden 1930's and the war-torn 1940's, consumer education passed through four distinct stages.[5]

1. *The exposé stage.* Muckrakers exposed the problems and pitfalls of the consumer in a series of books with titles like *Your Money's Worth, 100 Million Guinea Pigs, Chamber of Horrors,* and *Skin Deep.*

2. *The do-it-yourself stage.* Consumers were taught how to produce their own cosmetics, tooth powders, mouthwashes, and cleaning fluids.

[5] Edward Damon, "Consumer Education Rides Again," *The Clearing House,* 40:391–396 (March 1966).

3. *The testing stage.* Consumers Research, Consumers Union, and government testing agencies occupied a central position.

4. *The understanding and cooperative stage.* After the National Association of Secondary School Principals in cooperation with the National Better Business Bureau instituted a Consumer Education Study in 1942, attempts were made by consumers' organizations, business, and government to remove mutual distrust of consumers' groups and business. Better Business Bureaus are representative of this trend.

The Revival of Consumer Education: The Second Surge

Almost by default consumer education has reverted to other subject areas and especially to distributive education. By the middle of the 1960's, a remarkable revival of consumer education in our schools and by the government was under way. In 1963, the National Education Association stated that schools play an important role in teaching students to make more intelligent consumer choices. In fact, "the schools may provide the only unbiased education consumers encounter." [6] In the 1960's, the critical areas of consumer education are credit principles and practices, budgeting family income, money management, buying insurance, and the economics of health and medical care.

Since 1953, the Food and Drug Administration has a Division of Consumer Education. Its Consumer Information Branch prepares every type of media used in the FDA consumer program. It issues speech materials, pamphlets, exhibits, films, filmstrips, tapes, and radio and television scripts. Its special province is caring for the needs of schools, senior citizens, low-income groups, and foreign language groups. No one knows yet how long the new consumer-education movement will last in an economy in which most consumers are affluent by pre-World War II standards.

On the high school level, the reawakening of consumer education was heralded by the consumer-education program sponsored by the faculty of Lincoln High School in Yonkers, New York, assisted by the Consumers Union on the school's request. Beginning in 1962, the bits and pieces of consumer education which were being taught were coordinated to develop a comprehensive and effective consumer-education program for all students. The results at Lincoln High School included a faculty consumer-education committee, joint efforts on behalf of consumer education by seven academic departments, and assembly programs.

[6] National Education Association, *Education in a Changing Society.* Washington, D.C., National Education Association, 1963, p. 42.

In a leaflet entitled *The Consumer in the American Economy,* the Consumers Union pointed out that the need for consumer education is now greater than ever before. The product and brand explosion has brought some 8,000 items to large supermarkets, all different products, brands, and sizes. It is very difficult for the consumer to know which are the better values in terms of quality and price. Moreover, the packaging revolution induces the consumer to buy the package instead of the content. As silent salesmen, packages use color, design, shape, and special wrappings to induce people to part with their money. Planned and unplanned obsolescence makes a five-year-old automobile look like Noah's ark in the eyes of style-conscious teen-agers. In automobiles, the estimated total annual model changes over a twelve-year period was placed at $35 billion. Nutritional and medical quackery cost consumers an estimated one billion dollars per year. For example, Americans spend over half a billion dollars a year for vitamins, minerals, other supplements, and so-called health foods which they do not need. The average American family now spends approximately $18 a month ($216 a year) on nonprescription drugs or over-the-counter products. Many of these drugs bring little health benefit, and, for the most part, according to the American Medical Association, represent wasted dollars.

It is characteristic of Americans—as de Tocqueville noted over 125 years ago—to form associations to promote their pet reforms. Educators have been no exception. For a while, educators' consumer groups flourished and then died largely for lack of the unity that maintains single-discipline associations. Since the 1930's, consumer education has been a part of economics, business education courses, home economics, science, economic citizenship, or problems of democracy. The Institute for Economic Education and the Consumer Education Association, both established in 1937, boasted a membership of several hundred educators each. After their disappearance, no official consumers' organization for educators existed until 1953. In that year, twenty-two educators from various fields formed the Council on Consumer Information for the purpose of more effective fact-finding and teaching of consumer information.

Consumers' Rights and Obligations

As presented by President John F. Kennedy in his message to Congress on March 15, 1962, consumers' rights include the following.

1. *The right to safety*—to be protected against the marketing of goods which are hazardous to health or life
2. *The right to be informed*—to be protected against fraudulent, de-

ceitful, or grossly misleading information, advertising, labeling, or other practices, and to be given the facts he needs to make an informed choice

3. *The right to choose*—to be assured, wherever possible, access to a variety of products and services at competitive prices; and in those industries in which competition is not workable and government regulation is substituted, an assurance of satisfactory quality and service at fair prices

4. *The right to be heard*—to be assured that consumer interests will receive full and sympathetic consideration in the formulation of government policy, and fair and expeditious treatment in its administrative tribunals.

The obligations of consumers include the following.

1. Exercise better buymanship.
2. Demand only reasonable services, credit, and adjustments.
3. Join consumers' organizations, or at least take an interest in the literature on consumer problems supplied at low cost by governmental agencies.
4. Perform some home repair jobs themselves and be thrifty despite the temptations of this throw-away age.
5. Be prudent consumers by buying first things first (necessities and comforts before luxuries).

Consumer Economics in the Twelfth-Grade Course

One of the major purposes of teaching economics on the high school level should be to acquaint the students with the economic institutions of the students' world and the workings of these institutions. Taking into consideration the level of understanding of his class, the teacher should teach some analytical economics to all of his students—the average and the slow, as well as the bright—but he should always try to apply both the analytical tools and the models he develops to the experiences of the students encountered in their personal lives and within their life space. Consumer education copes with two universal real-life problems: buymanship and personal money management. The proponents of consumer education believe that it should be *required* for all high school students, whether college-bound, or dropout. Inasmuch as it deals with concrete, self-motivating situations in the marketplace, it is especially suited to our young people with the greatest unmet needs—the nonacademic and the disadvantaged. The purpose of education in buymanship and personal money management is to open up the possibility of getting more of what one believes contributes to the good life. Its purpose is not "to teach young people to buy less, to snuff out their dearest desires, and scrimp along in a miserly fashion." [7]

Consumer Economics for the College-Bound

Provided that he also treats consumers' rights and obligations just mentioned, the teacher may well use the approach, techniques, and subject matter outlined in the JCEE's *Economics and the Consumer* for his academic students.

The college-bound course in high school economics should stress the essential analysis, concepts, facts, and institutions involved in personal decision-making in a free-enterprise price system. It should analyze patterns of earning one's living and patterns of spending. It should emphasize consumer credit—that marvelous miracle that enables the consumer to enjoy next year's income this year—rational household budgeting, forms of saving, and true interest rates on installment purchases. It should also examine governmental sources of income and governmental patterns of spending, including governmental versus personal budget-making. The student will emerge from his study of the unit on the consumer with some idea of the interaction of the decisions made by the individual as an earner, spender, saver and taxpayer. These interactions can be illustrated visually by use of the circular-flow model involving decisions by the consumer, business, and government. Not only is the consumer unit well adapted to teaching statistical skills, models and basic concepts, but it also lends itself readily to case studies such as the effects of inflation or recession on earnings, saving, spending and taxing patterns.

Consumer Economics for the Terminal Student

For the slower student, for whom the high school course is terminal, a special course in economics should be developed to focus on the individual as consumer, producer, worker, taxpayer, and citizen.

The first ten lessons, devoted to a unit on the consumer, might bear the following titles.

[7] Fred T. Wilhelms, "Key to Many Doors," *The Bulletin of the National Association of Secondary School Principals* (October 1967), pp. 3–13.

1. How does the teen-ager spend his money?
2. How are prices determined?
3. What role does the consumer play in our economy?
4. Does the consumer get his money's worth?
5. How can the consumer be helped to secure better values?
6. How does insurance help the consumer?
7. How can the consumer best save, invest, and borrow?
8. How has our expanding economy raised the American standard of living?
9. Why is the American standard of living still rising?
10. Why is it in our interest to help people in other countries as well as in the United States to raise their living standards?

The terminal course, of course, can be enriched at all points by relating and applying each lesson to the personal needs and experiences of the student and his family.

Student Learning Activities in Consumer Education

The following activities, with the possible exception of critical book reviews, are suggested for both the college-bound and the terminal student.

1. *Practice in Buymanship*

Effective buymanship training requires active involvement on the part of your students. To spark interest in buymanship, ask your class to select an item that students very much want to buy, for example, a stereo tape recorder, and then encourage one student, or a committee of students, to engage in a vigorous shopping campaign involving window shopping, advertisements, labels and brand names, advice of friends, and information supplied by governmental and consumer testing agencies. In addition to the analysis involved, such a realistic shopping adventure will build up a set of specifications for electronic equipment and will result in the creation of a valuable vocabulary of useful terms.

2. *Analysis of Television Commercials*

Ask your students to tally the number of times the sponsor's brand name is mentioned in a favorite television program and to record the amount of time devoted to commercials. The students will be surprised to learn that mention of the brand name occurs on an average of more than one a minute in an hour-long program. In the discussion that follows, class and teacher can discuss, among other things, why many television programs are teen-oriented. Such a study serves as excellent motivation for an analysis of the benefits and evils of advertising.

3. *Critical Book Reviews*

Writing a critical, analytical book review is an excellent way for a student to broaden his mental horizons. A few books that will prod your students to analytical thinking are:

Black, Hillel, *Buy Now, Pay Later*. New York, William Morrow and Company, 1961.
Caplovitz, David, *The Poor Pay More*. New York, The Free Press, 1963.
Dacey, N. F., *What's Wrong with Your Life Insurance?* New York, Crowell, Collier and Macmillan, 1963.
Nader, Ralph, *Unsafe at Any Speed*. New York, Grossman, 1965.
Packard, Vance, *The Hidden Persuaders*, 1957; *The Waste Makers*, 1960. New York, David McKay Company.
Weir, Walter, *Truth in Advertising and Other Heresies*. New York, McGraw-Hill, 1963.

4. *An Analysis of Savings and Investment Programs*

A teacher can motivate this topic by posing a problem: "If you had $1,000 to invest, would you place your money in U.S. Savings Bonds, a savings account, real estate, or stocks and bonds? Explain your decision." "If you had $100,000 to invest, would you change your portfolio? How? Why?"

5. *Case Studies on Budgeting and Financial Planning*

The teacher may prepare descriptive paragraphs on the financial problems faced by Mr. and Mrs. Newlywed during their first year of marriage. A variety of topics suggest themselves: buying or renting a home, easy payment plans, impulsive buying versus budgeting, and financing the first baby. Each paragraph should be followed by questions leading to an analysis of the sources of their financial difficulties and requesting possible solutions to their problems.

6. *Use of Community Resources*

The possibilities regarding the use of community resources are legion. Visits to supermarkets, wholesalers, factories, stock exchanges or brokerage houses, and banks, and invitations to speakers representing financial institutions and government agencies are just a few that come readily to mind.

The Consumer-Oriented Course

A consumer-oriented course, which stresses personal economic problems, has both strengths and weaknesses.

On the plus side of the ledger are the following.

1. The course encompasses teachable topics, based for the most part on the developmental tasks of youth—drives that are intrinsically self-motivating.

2. The focus is on responsible economic citizenship—the high school student as a consumer, worker, union member, taxpayer, and future parent.

3. The approach humanizes the content of the course for terminal students and relates it to the daily life and the life space of the boys and girls.

4. It is a realistic course, geared to the students' needs, aspirations, and socioeconomic backgrounds, and tailored to their ability levels.

On the minus side, it raises two worrisome questions.

1. Is economic citizenship the only economics of which the terminal student is capable? As future voters who will participate in elections, terminal students will be called upon to decide economic issues at the ballot box on terms of equality with the college-bound. Will the terminal student be equipped with sufficient analytical insight to choose wisely?

2. Is life-adjustment education enough? Are we not gliding over the hard economic facts of life? The teachers must acquaint students with unpleasant facts. High school drop-outs constitute the greatest number of unemployed youth. The average industrial worker must be retrained several times during his working life because of the inroads of automation. Retraining programs and vocational education in the schools may be training youths for jobs that will be obsolete in the next decade.

The Implications of Consumer Economics

What, then, are the implications of consumer economics for the one-semester course usually given in the senior year of high school?

First, curriculum builders should view economics from a K–12 approach. It is to be hoped that a hierarchy of economic understandings and skills will gradually emerge which will be broadened, deepened, and escalated as the student progresses from grade to grade. As a consequence of planning, the one-semester course will reenforce, but not merely repeat for the nth time materials already taught in previous grades and other subjects.

Second, the personal-problems approach via consumer economics serves as a powerful motivational force. It has appeal to the teen-ager. Teen-agers are America's largest leisure class—and leisure classes are notorious spenders. The average teen-ager has a personal per capita income of $625, much of which is used for discretionary spending. One of the significant business trends of the twentieth century has been the campaign by the advertising agencies to capture the growing teen-age market. An army of researchers, market consultants, and psychologists is specializing in converting teen-age fads into cash receipts.

With pitfalls and temptation on every side, how can we deny a place to consumer economics in our high school curriculum? The consumer has had a time-honored place in the discipline. The father of all economists, Adam Smith, said "Consumption is the sole end and purpose of all production." In an affluent society, aspiring to be a Great Society, who can deny a place in the course of study to the favorite avocation of all?

Reference Shelf for Consumer Education

The best single source on the resurgence of consumer education is the October 1967 issue of *The Bulletin of the National Association of Secondary-School Principals*. Devoted exclusively to "Consumer Education: Its New Look," it discusses all aspects of the new consumers' movement stressing programs in action and the tools required to do a good teaching job. Edward Reich, a leader in the field and a veteran teacher of consumer education, describes the best of the textbooks, monographs, pamphlets, and periodicals in his article called "Reference Shelf in Consumer Economics." Other articles in this issue deal with the government and consumer education, the Council on Consumer Information, private testing agencies, and education in family finance.

Economics teachers will find the following sources indispensable:

Publications

1. *Consumer Education in Lincoln High School* (Consumers Union, Mount Vernon, New York) describes a schoolwide consumer-education program in action.
2. *Consumer Research* and *Consumer Reports,* the monthly magazines of Consumers Research and Consumers Union, respectively, together with their annual buying guides, will serve a multiplicity of uses.
3. *Consumers All,* the Yearbook of the U.S. Department of Agriculture, is an excellent, 500-page, clothbound source book in the problems of economic education both for novice and expert. (Price: $2.75. Write to The Superintendent of Documents, Washington, D.C. 20402.)

Bibliographies

1. *Check List* (Joint Council on Economic Education, 1212 Avenue of the Americas, New York, New York 10036) includes some economic materials applicable to consumer education.
2. *Consumer Information Price List* is a valuable bibliography of interesting consumer pamphlets printed by the government, many of which are free and most of which are obtainable at 25¢ or less. (Price: 10¢. Write to The Superintendent of Documents, Washington, D.C. 20402.)
3. *Free and Inexpensive Learning Materials* (Division of Field Services, George Peabody College for Teachers, Nashville, Tennessee) is a valuable source for all kinds of educational materials, including consumer education.

Business Organizations

The following business organizations produce millions of pamphlets each year on various aspects of consumer problems. Although they attempt to be objective, the publishers are "point of view" organizations with an understandable bias in favor of the activities of the business or group they represent.

Household Finance Corporation (Prudential Plaza, Chicago, Illinois 60601): filmstrips and leaflets on buymanship.

National Better Business Bureau (230 Park Avenue, New York, New York 10017): fact booklets on deceptive practices.

National Thrift Committee (121 West Wacker Drive, Chicago, Illinois 60601): leaflets on money management.

Institute of Life Insurance (277 Park Avenue, New York, New York 10017): pamphlets on health and life insurance from the insurance man's point of view.

National Association of Manufacturers (277 Park Avenue, New York, New York 10017): consult *Project Tips,* a clearing house for materials produced by its members, before writing to individual manufacturers.

13 Measurement and Evaluation in Economics

Measurement

Measurement is the act of making comparisons. It rests on quantification, that is, on a particular test score stated as a quantity, but such a score has no significance until it is compared with other scores. Measurement has four chief purposes.

1. To learn how the student ranks in relation to his group. In life situations, we are often required to take qualifying examinations: to teach, to become a barber, or to secure a driver's license. On College Board Examinations, the student is assigned a rank in relation to the other candidates.

2. To determine whether the student's level of achievement is equal to his potentialities. Such information is useful for guidance, formal or informal.

3. To utilize the results of tests to improve the teacher's own performance.

4. To furnish feedback in the form of test results which can reenforce learning, strengthen motivation, and motivate further study.

Evaluation

Evaluation is the process of gathering and interpreting all information that will give reliable and valid indications of changes in students' behavior. Evaluation is basically subjective. It involves the exercise of judgment. Several purposes are served by evaluation.

1. It can be used to diagnose student difficulties and provide guidance in preparing remedial instruction.

2. It can be used to estimate the efficacy of a method, or of a unit, and help to determine the grade placement of material.

3. It can appraise the value of a whole program, the effectiveness of a piece of equipment, the usefulness of programmed instruction, and even the merits of an individual teacher.

Evaluation Instruments

Economics teachers should be aware of the various types of evaluation instruments in use: observation, anecdotal records, conferences with students, case studies, role playing, sociometric methods, ratings by students, and cumulative records. Testing, measurement, and evaluation is too large a subject to be treated within the compass of a chapter of a book of this size. All textbooks on methods in the social studies devote a section to this important facet of the teacher's job. *Evaluation in Social Studies*, the Thirty-Fifth Yearbook of the National Council for Social Studies (1965), treats comprehensively all aspects of the field. It includes helpful chapters on "The Objective Test Item" and "Improving the Essay Test in the Social Studies."

Evaluation of Changes in Students' Attitudes

Have your students changed their attitudes or do they still slavishly follow the conventional wisdom on economic issues? By including on a test an opinion poll of the class on statements such as "An unbalanced budget is always bad," and "The TVA exemplifies 'creeping socialism'," the teacher can evaluate the progress toward rational analysis which his class has made. The poll might include categories such as "I agree," "I disagree," "I mildly disagree," "I strongly agree." Reasons for agreement or disagreement might be listed below the statement for the students to check. Since the object of the items is to evaluate student attitudes and not to award grades, the opinion poll might take the form of a bonus question for which all students, regardless of their answers, are awarded five or ten points. The value of the poll is further enhanced if some of the items are repeated on future tests for the purpose of comparison.

Teacher-Made Tests

Every classroom teacher is responsible for planning, giving, and interpreting his own teacher-made tests. To a large degree such tests serve two purposes: to secure marks for grading the students and to diagnose weaknesses in the instructor's teaching procedures. The student is also interested in his progress and in his rank in the class. Moreover, testing is one way—albeit an extrinsic way—of motivating the student to study. Diagnostic teaching helps the teacher to discover the things a student knows, or does not know, about economics. Guided by this knowledge, a teacher can undertake corrective and remedial help. Furthermore, the feedback of teacher-made tests measures the teacher's success in presenting meaningful learning experiences to his students. A conscientious teacher will therefore use test results to improve his own teaching effectiveness. An item analysis of each of your teacher-made tests will indicate the parts of the course which are least understood by the students. An examination of the incorrect responses can be helpful in determining the teaching techniques and materials which created false impressions in the minds of the students.

Beginning teachers soon learn that the construction of teacher-made tests is not easy. No teacher of economics can hope to duplicate the carefully worked out steps followed by testing experts, such as the Educational Testing Service or Science Associates, in preparing standardized objective-test items. Nor can a searching, valid diagnostic test be thrown together during a free period in the teachers' lounge. Test items, test ideas, and test questions should be assembled by the teacher as an outcome of each day's lesson planning and lesson presentation. It is good practice to place each item, idea, or question on an individual index card, then filed and kept for future reference at test time. No file is more of a time-saver than a questions file. Teachers should also file away good uniform examination questions (midterm, final or Regents). *Scholastic* magazines and similar student publications, *Time, The New York Times*, and other periodicals prepare end-term current affairs examinations that are a good source of examination questions.

Before preparing his test, the teacher must review the subject matter, principles, and concepts that he has taught, decide on the scope of the test, and the weight he intends to assign to each part. A classroom teacher will find his task less onerous if he follows a few simple rules.

Objective Test Items

In preparing objective items (multiple-choice, matching, true-false, completion), (1) plan the scope, purpose, and timing of your questions carefully, (2) provide a separate answer sheet and collect all copies of the test after the students have taken it (so you can use it again), (3) analyze the test results question by question to reveal to you areas that need reteaching, and (4) begin the file of good test questions (each on a separate card) for future use.

Examples of Multiple-Choice Questions

(   ) 1. Today economists measure the wealth of a country by (1) its developed natural resources (2) its gross national product (3) the total value of its foreign trade (4) the amount of gold and silver backing its currency.

(   ) 2. Which is characteristic of *both* capitalism and communism? (1) use of capital (2) a predominantly free-enterprise system (3) government ownership of major industries (4) planning of production by the central government.

(   ) 3. The term *escalator clause* in labor-management contracts refers to (1) union representation (2) working conditions (3) seniority rights (4) wage adjustments.

Examples of Completion Questions

1. If "too many dollars chase too few goods" there is a tendency for prices to _____.
2. The federal agency that serves as "the policeman of the stock exchange" is _____.
3. Rent is to land as interest is to _____.

Examples of True-False Questions

Directions: Indicate whether each of the following statements is true or false. If the statement is false, replace the word or phrase in *italic type* with one which will make it correct. Use the space provided for the purpose.

_____ 1. A deficit in our *balance of trade* causes a decrease in our gold reserves.

_____ 2. "Demand-pull" and "cost-push" refer to theories regarding causes of *inflation*.

———— 3. The right to use, dispose of, and bequeath the things one owns is called *freedom of enterprise.*

Examples of Matching Questions

For *each* graph outline in column A, select from column B, the *one* description of the data which the graph outline is intended to represent. In the space provided, place the *number* preceding the description you have selected.

Column A   *Column B*

(   ) 1.

(   ) 2.

(   ) 3.

1. Consumer prices for commodities, services, all items, 1960–1965

2. Deficit in the federal budget from 1962 to 1967

3. Retail sales of four classes of products in 1964 and 1967

4. Union membership in the total labor force, 1967

5. Per cent distribution of males by years of school completed, 1945, 1955, 1965

[In good matching questions, the items to be discriminated are similar; in this case they are graphs.]

The following checklists provide valuable criteria for constructing objective test items.

CHECKLIST FOR MULTIPLE-CHOICE ITEMS
1. Does the stem of the question contain the central problem?
2. Is the central problem stated succinctly?
3. Do you have at least four choices?
4. Have you included any choices that are obviously wrong?
5. Have you placed the foils at the end of the incomplete statement?
6. Have you scattered the correct responses?
7. Have you avoided, or at least minimized, negative responses?
8. Are your questions practical, pertinent, and realistic?
9. Have you used an illustration where one is clearly needed to present the central problem?
10. Have you avoided irrelevant clues?

CHECKLIST FOR MATCHING ITEMS

1. Have you included two or three extra choices from which the responses must be chosen?
2. Are the items tested homogeneous or at least related?
3. Have you arranged the selection column in logical order?
4. Are your directions specific?
5. Is the entire matching question on a single page?

CHECKLIST FOR TRUE-FALSE ITEMS

1. Have you avoided picayune items?
2. Have you avoided using negative items which are frequently misread?
3. Have you eliminated questions which repeat textbook statements?
4. Have you avoided including more than one point in one statement?
5. Have you simplified statements so that they will not be too long or too involved?
6. Have you excluded trick or catch questions that have no place in examinations?
7. Are all of your true items and false items of approximately the same average length?

Essay Questions

In preparing essay questions, (1) decide upon the kind of learning (analysis, problem solving, conceptual learning, skills, or facts) that you want to stress, (2) start questions with words and phrases like "compare," "contrast," or "argue for or against," (3) prepare a model answer for each question, and (4) before grading your papers read over several questions to get the feel of the responses. Read and grade all of the answers to the first question before going on to the second. Even in college, the blue book is used too frequently as a grading device that tests memory rather than understanding. As an alternative the teacher may occasionally use an open textbook and notebook type of examination.

Examples of Essay Questions

A. Compare the economic system of the United States and the Soviet economic system with respect to *each* of the following:
   a. Ownership and management of capital   (5)
   b. Competition in business and industry   (5)

　　c. Role of unions　　　　　　　　　　　　　　　(5)
　　d. Economic incentives　　　　　　　　　　　　(5)
　　　　　　　　Total—Twenty Credits
[Allot specific credit to each part of the essay question.]

B. Give an explanation that will *either* support or refute *each* of the following economic theories.

　　a. Shrinking profits will result in a diminished supply of money for investments.
　　b. A planned federal budget deficit will check a recession.
　　c. High protective tariffs result in high employment.
　　d. An increase in wages results in an increase in consumer prices.
　　e. Automation results in an increase in unemployment.

C. Dr. Martin Luther King has said that only a guaranteed annual income will eliminate poverty among Negroes and whites in the United States.

　　a. What does "a guaranteed annual income" mean?
　　b. Argue for or against the proposal endorsed by Dr. King.
　　c. Discuss *two* measures already undertaken by the Johnson Administration to alleviate poverty in our country.

The following checklist provides valuable criteria for constructing essay questions.

CHECKLIST FOR ESSAY TESTS

1. Have you chosen an area for major emphasis? facts? problem-solving? conceptual learning? application of principles?
2. Do your essay questions begin with directions such as "Compare," "Evaluate," and "Justify"?
3. Are your questions clearly stated in unambiguous everyday English?
4. Have you eliminated opinion questions, except as an indicator of student attitudes and values?
5. Will the students be able to answer the questions adequately in the time allotted?
6. Have you prepared a model answer?
7. Do your questions sample basic learnings or do they tap knowledge that is exotic or peripheral?
8. Do your questions test the ability to organize materials and ideas in a manner different from that in which the ideas or materials were originally taught?
9. Have you included skills such as the interpretation of graphs, charts, cartoons, or tests of the students' critical capacity?
10. Have you allocated fairly your credits for each part and sub-part of the examination?

Uniform Mid-Term and Final Examinations

In preparing for an important examination such as a mid-term test or a final examination, the teacher should write down and file away during the semester ideas for questions as they come to him. In fact, after each lesson the teacher should prepare questions based upon the material covered. Later, he can select those items which he wants to use in the mid-term or final examination, secure in the knowledge that he did indeed cover that material. Teachers who wait until the last minute to construct a mid-term or final often forget whether a given topic was covered, and therefore produce a test lacking in balance.

In drawing up mid-term and final examination questions, the teacher should keep the following in mind.

1. Determine the scope and nature of the test, that is, the key ideas, basic concepts, economic institutions, understandings, attitudes, and skills you wish to test. Decide in advance the credits you expect to assign to each major topic and subtopic.

2. Pay careful attention to the reading level of the test and to the clarity and precise meaning of each question.

3. Provide specific directions and give examples, if you are using unfamiliar varieties of objective questions.

4. Avoid using questions or statements taken directly from the textbook.

5. Avoid using negative items.[1]

6. Avoid the use of *always* or *never*.

7. Give a second person an opportunity to read and criticize your test items. If this procedure is not feasible, put the test aside for a cooling-off period before re-reading it.

8. Pay attention to ease of scoring. Overlay keys are excellent for short answer items and will save you a great deal of time in marking.

The Test of Economic Understanding

In 1963, a special Committee on the Measurement of Economic Understanding, composed of five well-known economists and leading educators, was established to devise a "Test of Economic Understanding," that would, in the eyes of professional economists and testing experts, help high school teachers to determine the degree of economic under-

---

[1] *Example:* Which of the following is not characteristic of free-enterprise capitalism? (1) freedom of contract (2) "imperfect" competition (3) government planning of economic life (4) private property.

standing achieved by high school students (with or without a formal course in high school economics). This test, sometimes known as the Stalnaker Test because Dr. John Stalnaker headed the committee, is the tool used by the Joint Council and its affiliates for pre- and post-testing to gauge progress in all of their programs.

Developed as the test was by leading economists, educational psychologists, and high school educators, the questions cover the basic areas of micro- and macroeconomics, plus questions on applied fields, such as international economics and comparative economic systems, but they omit all technical detail beyond such simple concepts as supply and demand. While there are a few factual questions, most are focused on the understanding of basic concepts and the ability to handle problem and application situations. A few call for analysis of major policy issues such as monetary and fiscal policy and/or the reading and interpretation of graphs and economic time series. Each question was pretested on thousands of students; many questions were extensively revised and the test carefully balanced as to coverage, degree of difficulty, and kinds of understanding. Barbara A. Peace states in *Evaluation in Social Studies* that "the level of understanding required is not very high, but appears to be appropriate for an introductory course—particularly a high school-level one."

Making Up Marks

The two aspects of teaching that worry teachers most are, first, classroom management and discipline, and, second, testing, grading, and evaluating student performance. Both are reported directly or indirectly to parents. Both are also intimately related to the teacher's success. The following items are useful in determining a student's grade.

1. The evidence in the form of marks supplied by written tests and examinations
2. The evidence furnished by term papers, position papers, oral reports, participation in panels, and special activities such as viewing and reporting on selected television programs or visiting places of economic interest
3. The quality and the extent of participation in class
4. The marking policies of the school

In sum, testing, measurement, and evaluation should be viewed as means of improving one's personal teaching program as well as measuring changes in attitudes, skills, and understandings on the part of one's students.

PART
III

Preparation for Teaching Analytical Economics

In order to accomplish the goals of course improvement, we need a secondary school teaching staff with greater competency in economics. Sad to relate, most social studies teachers are afraid to teach economics.

Albert Alexander,
Challenge, March 1964.

CHAPTER

14 *Preparation*
for Teaching
Economics

The Need for Specialization

The "faltering heart" of the problem of economic education is the
teacher unequipped to teach economic understanding because of his
own inadequate background in economics. Most of the efforts to improve teacher competence up to the late 1960's have been in the field of
in-service training. Psychologists believe that an economics teacher who
takes in-service courses and who attends economics workshops im-
proves his self-image. If the teacher sees himself as being informed and
capable in economics, he is likely to be a better teacher of the subject. A
secure teacher will innovate and experiment confidently and accept
evaluation realistically. Effective in-service training provides a rich and
extensive background of knowledge in economics. When such training
has been assimilated, the teacher is better equipped to provide learning
experiences, answer student questions, change classroom procedures,
and allow the freedom necessary for students to learn by discovery and
inquiry.

What constitutes adequate preparation for teaching economic understandings in the schools? To answer this question we must first survey
the market. Economic ideas are dispensed by three groups of teachers
in American schools. The most numerous consists of the K–6 elementary-school teachers in self-contained, nonspecialized classrooms, who
encounter economic ideas in social studies and the language arts. Next
come social studies teachers in specialized, grade 7–12 classes, who
teach economics-related subjects such as history, geography, government or business education, all of which include some economic
concepts and information. In a few instances, of course, the economics
content may be taught as economics in a solid 6- to 10-week unit within

United States History, American Government, Problems of Democracy, or a similar social studies course. Only a small percentage of American teachers teach the one-semester, twelfth-grade economics course as a separate discipline.

What should be the general nature of such a course? Let us quote Aristotle on this point:

Every systematic science, the humblest and noblest alike, seems to admit of two kinds of proficiency, one of which may properly be called scientific knowledge of the subject, while the other is a kind of educational acquaintanceship with it.

The objective of both a tailored course for teachers and the high school course for students should clearly be the inculcation of a good reading knowledge of economics within a liberal arts framework. A century and a quarter ago, when the British weekly, *The Economist,* was founded, the name meant a pragmatist, not a specialist in political economy. Alexander insists that the economic concepts taught the high school boy and girl must "fall within the common sense purview of the students." For pedagogical and psychological reasons, both the high school course and the tailored teachers' course must be built on their own experiences in the real world. In short, the tailored course that is preparing teachers to teach the one-semester high school course in economics cannot sacrifice economic institutions, descriptive approaches, and personal economic problems on the altar of principles and analysis.

College Preparation for Teaching Economics

What constitutes adequate preparation for teaching economic understandings in the public elementary and high schools? Before we attempt to answer this query, a quick survey of the college teaching of elementary economics is in order. Currently there is a wide divergence of opinion among economics professors as to the kind of economics that should be stressed in the elementary college course. Should the basic course attempt primarily to promote good economic citizenship? Should the freshman course be taught as part of the students' general cultural background in the liberal arts tradition? Should elementary economics basically be a useful background course for future businessmen, lawyers, and engineers? Or, should introductory economics be taught as a professional discipline?

Too often the view prevails that economics should be kept pure and undefiled. In brief, the professional economist jealously guards economics as an academic discipline with a body of rigorous theory which must be mastered if the student is to enjoy the essence of the subject. In the view of the economist, abstraction is the heart of economics. Although college students may find economics boring, dull, and abounding in generalizations which do not appear to match the reality of the economic world around them, the academician resists teaching institutional or applied economics. Although no more than 10 to 15 percent of all college undergraduates ever become economics majors, and only 2 to 3 percent of these students go on to graduate training in economics, the typical university economics professor treats each freshman as a potential doctoral candidate, who must master the analytical tools of the economist and the structure of the discipline. In the opinion of high school teachers, the abstract, analytical, highly structured elementary-principles undergraduate course and the graduate courses in economics, regardless of their merit, provide little or no help for most basic teacher needs at the secondary level. Obviously, prospective high school teachers and teachers already in service long for a course designed specifically to meet the needs of economic *educators* rather than *economists*.

In November 1966, *College Preparation for Teaching Economics*, the Report and Recommendations of an Advisory Seminar to the California Department of Education, suggested that all elementary school teachers and secondary school teachers of social studies should be required to take a basic economics course stressing economic reasoning, fundamental concepts and models, and applications to problem and policy situations. The basic three-semester-hours course would be supplemented by a one-semester-credit-hour classroom laboratory for case work on economic materials. In the classroom laboratory, future teachers would learn how to apply the economics learned to actual teaching situations. Ideally, this hour should be the joint effort of representatives of the department of economics and the school of education. The content and the pedagogical courses would be taken concurrently.[1]

The nature of the basic course is revealed by its objectives:

1. To stimulate an awareness of the major economic problems in our society

2. To provide for all students a firm understanding of the basic analytical concepts and principles (in the form of models) that will enable them to analyze major economic problems. This implies the elimination

---

[1] Advisory Seminar to the California State Department of Education, *College Preparation for Teaching Economics: Report and Recommendations*. New York, Joint Council on Economic Education, 1966, pp. 1–13. (Reprinted by permission of the California Department of Education.)

of much of the more elaborate, technical aspects of economic theory often included in elementary economics courses

3. To develop a rational objective way of thinking about and solving economic problems

4. To foster proficiency in using and evaluating qualitative and quantitative evidence, especially when conflicting views of economic problems are presented

5. In order to accomplish these objectives, at least one fourth of all class time should be devoted to applications and problems which are relevant to voters, sellers of services, and home managers

Elementary-school teachers would be required to take only the basic economics course and the classroom laboratory. As the Summary of Guidelines indicates, the requirements for social studies teachers would be higher.

SUMMARY OF GUIDELINES
A. For all teachers, K–12
    The Basic Course, three semester hours, stressing:
        1. Economic reasoning
        2. Basic concepts and models
        3. Applications to problem and policy situations
    Plus a "classroom laboratory" course in teaching economics.
B. For all social studies teachers, grades 7–12

A Basic Course sequence in economics	9	semester hours
1. The Basic Course	3	" "
2. Contrasting Economic Systems	3	" "
3. An elective, preferably an advanced problems course	3	" "

C. For teachers of the one-semester high school course

A minor in economics	21	semester hours
1. The Basic Course	3	" "
2. Contrasting Economic Systems	3	" "
3. Macroeconomics and Policy	3	" "
4. Microeconomics and Policy	3	" "
5. Quantitative Methods	3	" "
6. Two electives in economic problems	6	" "

Of course, any recognized university or college major in economics is acceptable, particularly if it includes, deepens, and expands the requirements for the minor set forth above. Laurence Leamer, a member of the seminar, suggested as the culmination a senior seminar in economics and economic education, one which would be concerned with basic questions of the nature and role of economics, including its educational role. "Economic philosophy and philosophy of economic education are essential," he said, "to a general educational experience for future teachers of economics." [2]

Adoption of Advanced Placement Programs "foreshadows the time when the upgrading of teacher preparation to a major in economics may be desirable for the high school course in economics." In the meantime, the seminar recommended that a major in economics will be a reasonable minimum of preparation for teaching in the Advanced Placement Program in Economics.[3]

A College Course for Teachers in Service

1. *Rationale of the Course*

In 1967, the New York City Council on Economic Education designed a course entitled *Economics for High School Teachers of Social Studies* to meet the needs of economics teachers in service.[4] The course is an outgrowth of a recent study entitled "The Economics Backgrounds of Social Studies Teachers in New York City's Public Schools," conducted by the Council. This survey indicated that years have passed since some social studies teachers have studied economics; that many teachers feel the need for strengthening their skills in the discipline; and that of the 986 social studies teachers polled, 80 percent showed interest in taking a specially tailored economics course, provided that it was subsidized. Furthermore, the introduction of a new Grade-Twelve Course in Economics, which emphasizes analysis, has heightened the need for a special college-level economics course for social studies teachers.

The proposed course is designed to meet the needs of all social studies teachers who desire greater knowledge of economic analysis, simple economic models, and the structure of the discipline. Although the course is designed with the needs of the one-semester twelfth-grade course in mind, all social studies teachers will profit by the institutional and analytical background provided for teaching the economic components of world regional studies, world and American history, and problems of democracy.

[2] *Ibid.*, p. 9.
[3] *Ibid.*, p. 11.
[4] The tailored course was prepared at the request of the Program Committee of the New York City Council on Economic Education by Dr. Bernard Newton, Professor of Economics, Long Island University, and by the author.

2. *Objectives of the Course*

a. To strengthen the analytical abilities of social studies teachers by developing an understanding of key analytical concepts and institutions conducive to thinking about and solving economic problems in a rational, objective way.

b. To enlarge the boundaries of the social studies teacher's factual knowledge in the discipline.

c. To foster proficiency in using and evaluating qualitative and quantitative evidence.

d. To enhance the capacities of social studies teachers to present economic facts and concepts in ways that are meaningful and which will capture the interest of high school age boys and girls.

3. *Approach to the Course*

The central theme of the course is the study of the principal institutions and problems of modern American capitalism. Some other significant economic systems are examined in order to enhance the understanding of the American system. Unlike the traditional survey-type college principles course, an underlying motif of the course is the more effective teaching of economics both in the new Grade-Twelve Economics Course and in the various social studies courses (American Studies, World Studies, and Problems of Democracy). Since the course is limited to fifteen two-hour sessions, formal economic analysis of the type found in collegiate elementary principles courses would be inappropriate. Instead, the course will be geared to actual classroom situations that confront social studies teachers. The economic concepts, institutions, and facts of the course will be used to buttress analysis and to make it more meaningful. All parts of the course are designed to reenforce previous learning. At present, economics, as a high school subject, is probably able to conceptualize its basic theoretical framework more effectively than other social studies. The instructor will try to demonstrate the advantages of the conceptual approach to teaching economic understandings on grade levels nine through twelve.

4. *Scope and Structure*

The seven themes of the twelfth-grade one-semester New York City economics course and the economic components of the other social studies are regrouped into three major themes which characterize American capitalism. The three themes are:

I. The Fundamental Nature of Economics and of Economic Systems

The introductory theme deals with the nature of economics and other social sciences, highlighting the idea of system and economic systems.

II. Modern American Capitalism: Institutions, Mechanism, Problems, and Policy

The second theme places emphasis on the essence of the three main institutions of American capitalism—labor unions, corporations, and government—to ascertain the functions they perform in society. Imperfect competition turns the spot light on the market mechanism with its models of the firm and supply and demand. Theme II, which constitutes the analytical heart of the teachers' course, stresses income-expenditure analysis. The persistent problems outlined in the one-semester twelfth-grade course for students serve as a guide to the specific topics treated in the teachers' course. The topics which the students study include the maintenance of relative price stability; the market power of big business and big labor; economic insecurity (including poverty); and balance of payments problems. In discussing national economic goals and public policy, both practical and theoretical solutions will be examined.

III. Comparison of Some Significant Economic Systems: Growth and Development

The third theme compares the Soviet and the mixed economies such as those of Great Britain, France, or Sweden with our own. A subtheme on the industrialization of developing countries is used to introduce questions of infrastructure and internal and external aid. All three themes are, of course, taught with an eye on the working of the American system.

An outline of the teachers' course, indicating some of the topics that can be explored under each theme and the book(s) appropriate to each, follows:

ECONOMICS FOR TEACHERS OF HIGH SCHOOL SOCIAL STUDIES

THEME I.   Nature of Economics and the Other Social Sciences
           A. Nature of Economics and the Other Social Sciences
           B. Concept of a System and of Economic Systems
           C. The Universal Functions of Economic Systems
THEME II. Modern American Capitalism: Institutions, Mechanism, Problems and Policy
           A. Principal Institutions
              1. Labor unions
              2. Corporations
              3. Government
                 a. Political institutions used to attain economic and social goals

          b. Means to attain economic goals
    B. The Market Mechanism of Modern Capitalism
        1. Interrelationships of supply and demand
        2. Imperfect competition: monopolistic markets
        3. Income-expenditure analysis: determining short-run income levels
    C. Persistent Economic Problems of Modern American Capitalism
        1. The maintenance of adequate rates of economic growth
        2. The business cycle
        3. The maintenance of relative price level stability
        4. Market power of big business and big labor
        5. Personal economic insecurity and the problem of poverty
        6. Urban economic problems
        7. Balance of trade problems
    D. National Economic Goals and Public Policy
        1. National economic goals
        2. Monetary policy
        3. Fiscal policy
        4. Policy designed to control concentrations of market power

THEME III. Some Significant Economic Systems
    A. The Soviet Economy: Decision Making, Achievements, and Recent Trends
    B. Mixed Economies of Democratic Nations of Western Europe (Great Britain or France or Sweden)
    C. The Formation of Industrially Developed Economic Systems
        1. Institutional requisites for industrialization
        2. Problems and policies of underdeveloped economies
        3. The role of external assistance
          a. Industrialized economies
          b. International agencies
    D. Comparisons among Economic Systems
        1. Institutional mechanisms
        2. Welfare, wealth, and economic growth

5. *Suggested Reading*

THEME I. An excellent book on this theme is Robert L. Heilbroner's *Making of Economic Society*. Alfred R. Oxenfeldt and Vsevolod Holubnychy's *Economic Systems in Action* (3rd ed.) also has a fine chapter on this theme.

THEME II. For Topic B, Heilbroner has some good chapters, and Howard J. Sherman's *Growth, Employment and Inflation* is appropriate for Topic C. For Topic D, Arthur M. Okun's *Battle Against Unemployment* has pertinent readings. Heilbroner and Sherman also have good supporting chapters. For problems of the last two decades see Alvin H. Hansen's *Economic Issues of the 1960's* and Harold G. Vatter's *U.S. Economy in the 1950's*.

THEME III. Oxenfeldt and Holubnychy provide good material for the study of the United States, the Soviet Union, and France. The second edition also treats Great Britain.

Self-Improvement in Economic Education

In *Social Education,* April 1966, George L. Fersh, Assistant Director of the Joint Council on Economic Education, presented a detailed program of "Self-Improvement in Economic Education." Dr. Fersh pointed out that self-evaluation is the first step. He suggested that the teacher could discover his inadequacies in economics by taking "The Test of Economic Understanding," and further check his degree of economic literacy by reading *Economic Education in the Schools* (the Task Force Report). The teacher may also investigate the table of contents of recent college textbooks and test his grasp of economic analysis by reading articles dealing with economic issues presented in leading news weeklies, such as *Business Week*.

An economics teacher can, of course, fill in the gaps by independent reading (see Chapter 11), through courses such as summer economic-education workshops at universities co-sponsored by the JCEE and local regional economic councils, and numerous institutes on economic education at collegiate institutions under grants from the U.S. Office of Education and the National Science Foundation.

Still another way of filling gaps in economic understanding is through experiences in one's own community. Field trips to local enterprises should be undertaken by the teacher with specific questions in mind regarding the production and marketing activities of the business, its history, its employee-management relations, and its relationship to government. Part-time employment in a business will also provide an economics teacher with practical experience.

Perhaps the best way to fill the gaps in one's own economic understanding is the experience of teaching the one-semester high school course. By using a different college economics textbook as a background book each semester, the teacher not only equips himself to explain the subject to others in greater depth and to handle questions raised by the students but also contributes immeasurably to his own understanding of the discipline.

After following the foregoing suggestions for self-improvement in economics for a year or two, the teacher should make a progress check. For this purpose, he should use the self-evaluation suggestions offered earlier in this chapter. If the teacher now feels at ease with all of the media suggested, he has indeed gone a long way on the road to the mastery of economics.

In *The Economist as Teacher*, Laurence E. Leamer says, "Good economics teaching results most often from *trying* to be good." Good teaching depends on several things.

First, scholarship. *The Handbook for Social Studies Teaching*, published by the Association of Teachers of Social Studies of New York City, puts it simply: "There is no technique of classroom legerdemain that can take the place of scholarly competence." There is no substitute for a good command of the basics of economics as an academic discipline.

Second, dedication. Good teaching requires a great deal of time and energy for conferring with students; thinking up stimulating and appropriate motivations, questions, and applications; preparing a stimulating and challenging lesson; perfecting an examination; and keeping abreast of the latest developments in economic education through reading.

Third, "divine discontent." A good economics teacher never rests on his oars. He uses the principle of opportunity costs because in the economics of teaching he must constantly make choices as to approaches, methods, and materials. He continually experiments and evaluates, introduces new ideas and discards the old. He cannot make a good set of lesson plans and then use them over and over. "In successful teaching," Leamer says aptly, "there is no end of the road."

CHAPTER

15 *Additional Reading and Study Materials and Teacher Aids*

The following items represent a highly selective list of materials and aids for the teacher. Since reliable annotations are available in a number of sources mentioned in these pages, and since some have already been evaluated in this book, there is no need to duplicate such efforts. Economic literacy, as a never-ending process, demands ever-changing reading lists. At best, these short lists are merely springboards for jumping off into some current economic depths. The teacher of economics will find that he must soon construct his own springboards for greater coverage.

Books on Social Studies Methods

Association of Teachers of Social Studies of New York City, *Handbook for Social Studies Teaching*. New York, Holt, Rinehart and Winston, Inc., 1967. 370 pp.

Fenton, Edwin, *Teaching the New Social Studies in Secondary Schools: An Inductive Approach*. New York, Holt, Rinehart and Winston, Inc., 1966. 526 pp.

Fraser, Dorothy McClure, and Edith West, *Social Studies in Secondary Schools: Curriculum and Methods*. New York, Ronald Press, 1961. 476 pp.

Gross, Richard E., and Leslie D. Zeleny, *Educating Citizens for Democracy: Curriculum and Instruction in Secondary Schools*. New York, Oxford University Press, 1958. 591 pp.

High, James, *Teaching Secondary School Social Studies.* New York, Wiley, 1962. 481 pp.

Hunt, Maurice P., and Lawrence Metcalf, *Teaching High School Social Studies.* New York, Harper and Row, 1955. 471 pp.

Kenworthy, Leonard S., *Guide to Social Studies Teaching in Secondary Schools.* 2nd ed. Belmont, California, Wadsworth Publishing Co., 1966. 399 pp.

Leinwand, Gerald, and Daniel Feins, *Teaching History and the Social Studies in Secondary Schools.* New York, Pitman Publishing Corporation, 1967. 470 pp.

Lewenstein, Morris, *Teaching Social Studies in Junior and Senior High School.* New York, Rand-McNally, 1963. 556 pp.

McLendon, Jonathan C., *Social Studies in Secondary Education.* New York, Macmillan, 1965. 556 pp.

Quillen, I. James, and Lavone Hanna, *Education for Social Competence.* Chicago, Scott, Foresman, 1961. 536 pp.

Wesley, Edgar B., and Stanley P. Wronski, *Teaching Social Studies in High Schools.* Boston, Heath, 1964. 628 pp.

Economic Education: Problems and Materials

Advisory Seminar to the California State Department of Education, *College Preparation for Teaching Economics: Report and Recommendations.* New York, Joint Council on Economic Education, 1967. 15 pp.

Alexander, Albert (ed.), *Teaching Economics.* Bureau of Secondary Curriculum Development, New York State Education Department, 1962. 266 pp.

Association for Supervision and Curriculum Development, *Educating for Economic Competence.* Washington, D.C., ASCD Department of the NEA. 78 pp.

Bach, G. L., *Interpretive Manual and Discussion Guide for a Test of Economic Understanding.* Chicago, Science Research Associates, 1964. 36 pp.

Dawson, George G. (ed.), *Economic Education Experiences of Enterprising Teachers.* New York, Joint Council on Economic Education. Annually. 100 pp.

Frankel, M. L., *Economic Education.* New York, The Center for Applied Research in Education, Inc., 1965. 118 pp.

Haley, Bernard F., *Experiments in the Teaching of Basic Economics.* New York, Joint Council on Economic Education, 1967. 36 pp.

Joint Council on Economic Education, *Economics and the Consumer.* New York, Joint Council on Economic Education, 1966. 40 pp.

Joint Council on Economic Education, *Teachers Guide to Developmental Economic Education Program,* in two parts. New York, Joint Council on Economic Education, 1964.

> Part One: *Economic Ideas and Concepts—Based on the Task Force Report,* by James D. Calderwood. 46 pp.

> Part Two: *Suggestions for Grade Placement and Development of Economic Ideas and Concepts.* 95 pp.

Joint Council on Economic Education, *Economic Topics.* New York, Joint Council on Economic Education, 1964, 1965, 1966, 1967. 100 pp.

Joint Economic Committee, Subcommittee on Economic Progress, Ninetieth Congress of the United States, First Session, *Hearings: Economic Education.* Washington, D.C.; Government Printing Office, 1967. 2 vols.

Knopf, K. A., and J. H. Stauss (eds.), *The Teaching of Elementary Economics.* New York, Holt, Rinehart and Winston, 1960. 269 pp. (This book is aimed at the college level, but it has many useful ideas for the teacher of high school economics.)

National Task Force on Economic Education, *Economic Education in the Schools.* New York, Committee for Economic Development, 1961. 85 pp.

Special Textbook Study Committee, *Economics in the Schools.* A supplement to *The American Economic Review,* Vol. LIII, No. 1, Part 2, March 1963. 28 pp.

Wagner, Lewis E., *What Are Economic Problems?* Iowa City, Iowa, Bureau of Business and Economic Research, State University of Iowa, 1958. 19 pp.

Bibliographies

Annotated Bibliography of Economics Textbooks. Study units and films for use in high schools, Ohio Council on Economic Education. Athens, Ohio, Ohio University, 1964. 8 pp.

Annotated Bibliography of Materials in Economic Education. New York, Joint Council on Economic Education.

Bibliography of Pamphlet Materials, Economic Resources Center, Ypsilanti, Michigan, Eastern Michigan University Library, 1964. 29 pp.

Center for Economic Education, New York University, *A Description of High School Economics Text Books.* New York, Center for Economic Education, New York University, 1965. 16 pp.

Dawson, George G., *A List of Works on Teaching the Social Studies.* New York, Center for Economic Education, New York University, 1967. 24 pp.

Joint Council on Economic Education, *100 Selected Films in Economic Education.* New York, Joint Council on Economic Education, 1960. 34 pp.

Leamer, Laurence E., and Percy L. Guyton, *Suggestions for a Basic Economics Library.* New York, Joint Council on Economic Education. Annually. 60 pp.

Sayre, J. Woodrow, *Paperbound Books in Economics.* Albany, New York, New York State Council on Economic Education. Annually. 50 pp.

Audio-Visual Materials

The American Economy TV Films, NET Film Service, Audio-Visual Center, Bloomington, Indiana, Indiana University. (160 films.) Also available is *Highlights of the American Economy,* a specially selected set of 60 of these films.

Bibliography of Audio-Visual Aids. Ann Arbor, Michigan, Michigan Council on Economic Education, 1965. 57 pp.

Exploring Basic Economics. New York, Modern Learning Aids. Six films: *The Need for Economic Education; Everyday Economic Terms; The Anatomy of Free Enterprise; Productivity—Key to Progress; Foreign Trade—Challenge of a Changing World; Profits, Capital Equipment, and Economic Growth.*

Sloan Foundation and the National Association of Secondary School Principals, *The Modern Corporation,* produced by Sutherland Films.

The United States Economy in Action. Joint Council on Economic Education. Five filmstrips in color with manual: *Role of the Commercial Banking System; Role of the Federal Reserve System; Role of Consumers; Role of Our Labor Force; Our Growing America.*

Keeping Abreast of the Latest Statistics

Board of Governors, Federal Reserve System. *Federal Reserve Bulletin.* Monthly.

Bureau of the Budget. *The Federal Budget in Brief.* Annual.

Bureau of the Census. *Historical Statistics of the United States.* Washington, D.C., Government Printing Office, 1960. 789 pp.

Bureau of the Census. *Statistical Abstract of the United States*. Washington D.C., Department of Commerce. Biannual.

Bureau of Labor Review. *Monthly Labor Review*. Department of Labor. Monthly.

Bureau of Labor Statistics. *Economic Forces in the U.S.A. in Facts and Figures*. Department of Labor. Annual.

Colm, Gerhard, and Theodore Geiger, *The Economy of the American People*. Washington, D.C., National Planning Association, 1967. 220 pp.

Council of Economic Advisers. *Economic Indicators*. Washington, D.C., Government Printing Office. Monthly.

Council of Economic Advisers. *Annual Report to the President*. (Includes statistical appendix of approximately 100 pages.)

Joint Economic Committee of Congress. *Joint Economic Report*. Washington, D.C., Government Printing Office. Annual.

National Industrial Conference Board, Inc. *The Economic Almanac*. Biannual. *Glossary of Economic Terms* (1962) is a reprint from this publication.

Office of Business Economics. *Survey of Current Business*. Department of Commerce. Monthly.

Organizations Active in Publishing Economic Materials

American Economic Association. Northwestern University, Evanston, Illinois 60201.

American Federation of Labor and Congress of Industrial Organizations. 815 Sixteenth Street, N.W., Washington, D.C. 20006.

Committee for Economic Development. 711 Fifth Avenue, New York, New York 10022.

Federal Reserve Banks. Publications are issued by each of the 12 Federal Reserve District Banks.

Institute of Labor and Industrial Relations and the College of Education. University of Illinois, Urbana, Illinois 61801.

Joint Council on Economic Education, 1212 Avenue of the Americas, New York, New York 10036. Check with this organization for the name and address of your local council on economic education which also may provide you with helpful materials and aids.

National Association of Manufacturers. 2 East 48 Street, New York, New York 10017.

National Industrial Conference Board, Inc. 845 Third Avenue, New York, New York 10022.

New York State School of Industrial and Labor Relations. Cornell University, Ithaca, New York 14850.

United States Chamber of Commerce. 1615 N. Street, N.W., Washington, D.C. 20006.